SOFT FURNISHINGS

SOFT FURNISHINGS

IDEAS AND FABRICS BY DESIGNERS GUILD

ORBIS PUBLISHING · LONDON

Editor Elsie Burch Donald

Art Editors Jill Leman Muriel Mackenzie

Principal photographer Bruce Wolf

Technical Consultant Lindsay Vernon

Writers Deborah Evans Anne Hulbert

Valerie Jackson Lindsay Vernon

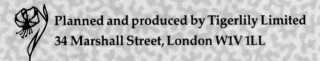 **Planned and produced by Tigerlily Limited**
34 Marshall Street, London W1V 1LL

Published 1980 by Pan Books Ltd.,
Cavaye Place, London SW10 9PG
and simultaneously in hardback by
Orbis Publishing Limited
20–22 Bedfordbury,
London WC2
2nd printing 1981

© Tigerlily Ltd., 1980

Printed and bound in Great Britain by
Fakenham Press Limited, Fakenham, Norfolk

ISBN 0 85613 277 2

Contents

Introduction

Soft furnishing is about fabrics – their colours, textures, designs and uses; the way they can be cut, sewn and put together to create comfortable yet imaginative surroundings. This book shows some of my favourite rooms and illustrates how different patterns and colours can be used together. I believe that some of the best ideas are simple ones and that is why my company, Designers Guild, presents a range of fabrics, wallpapers, furniture and accessories but, to some extent, leaves it to the customer's own design sense to put together an individual look. I think that most people have more design sense than they're given credit for. What frightens them is the mystique surrounding the whole idea of interior design, so I have tried to do the 'spadework' – both in my shops and through the ideas presented here – and readers may be pleasantly surprised to see how different scales of design and pattern can be combined successfully, provided there is some unifying influence. This book also shows in detail how to make soft furnishings and there are many ideas for improvisation: how to convert an inexpensive cane chair into something more special by 'upholstering' the seat and back; how a cheap chipboard base can become a pretty table by covering it with an embroidered or appliqued cloth. Even beginners should be able, with a little imagination and patience, to get professional-looking results by following the instructions and diagrams. Another use of the book is learning to do repairs: these are expensive nowadays and so it is an advantage to know how to mend tattered upholstery and curtains. My aim therefore is twofold, to illustrate the practical aspects of soft furnishings and at the same time to stimulate readers' own ideas.

TRICIA GUILD

Household linens

Most household linen is simple to make as it is cut from rectangles of cloth on the straight grain and only needs straight seams and plain hems. Embellishment can be added according to personal taste: table linen makes a particularly good setting for embroidery and bed linen can be decoratively finished with scalloped edges or embroidered borders.

FABRICS

The term 'linen' is really a misnomer because real linen is expensive, not readily available and not very easy to take care of. More suitable fabrics are cotton or cotton/polyester mixtures and acrylics. Since fabrics must withstand constant washing they should be strong and colourfast. They should be easy to iron or in a fibre or finish which does not need ironing.

Table 'linen'. Dress or soft furnishing fabrics can be used or purpose-made fabrics can be bought from specialist needlework shops (particularly desirable if embroidery is to be added or the edges hemstitched).

Bedspreads. The soft furnishing department of a good store is the best place to look for suitable fabric for bedspreads. Ask for advice if the fabrics are not labelled with recommended washing instructions and recommended uses.

Bed 'linen'. Sheeting by the metre or yard is made in pure cotton and cotton/polyester mixture in two standard widths – 230cm (90in) for double beds and 178cm (70in) for single beds. If only the wider size is obtainable then trim off the excess to make a single sheet and use the spare fabric for pillowcases. It is not advisable to use fabrics other than sheeting for bed linen, although for pram pillowcases you could use a good quality dress fabric such as *broderie anglaise*.

Wide fabrics. It should be possible to buy appropriate fabric wide enough to make coverings for most tables and beds. But if the fabric has to be joined to make the right width, try to position the seam so that it is unobtrusive or adds in some way to the overall design. Braids or bands of contrasting fabric can be stitched on to cover the seamline or a strip of lace could be stitched between the edges.

For calculating fabric amounts when you have to make joins, see in the Sewing Guide.

Household linen can be of simple, straight-forward construction or can be embellished with decorative edgings.

The bedspread above combines the methods of simple quilting and making a throw-over bedspread, both of which are described in this chapter. The gathered skirt, or valance, softens the line of the quilted spread while hiding the frame and legs.

The pair of pillowcases on the right are made by the one-section method described on page 24. They have an inside pocket which holds the pillow in position. This style of pillowcase is the simplest to make and is probably the most popular.

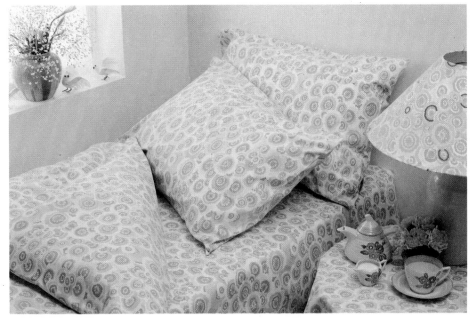

A wide border in a contrasting fabric characterizes the pillowcase style opposite. The border has mitred corners and is made separately and then sandwiched between the back and front sections of a conventional three-section case.

The zigzag embroidery stitch round the outer edges of this pair of pillowcases eliminates conventional seams and, at the same time, creates a highly decorative edge.
The fitted bottom sheet and continental quilt cover are made following instructions on pages 20 and 21.

Tablemats, like napkins, can be made from hemmed rectangles of fabric but the version shown here is both a useful and visually pleasing variation on the conventional theme.

Thin wadding is 'sandwiched' between two layers of fabric and the backing fabric, which is cut larger, is folded forward with mitred corners, to make a border. Raw edges are covered with decorative zigzag stitching and pretty cut-out motifs are applied to the four corners and to the napkins.

Printed fabric often needs only the
simplest style of construction to make a
decorative addition to a room. Sufficient
effect can come from the pattern and
the colours, and this can be enlarged
by combining different prints.
The tablecloth and napkins (above)
are made in the same fabric, but the
napkin round the wine bottle and the
chair cushions are made in different
prints. This combination of blues
provides interest on its own but it also
performs the more important function
of making a muted background for the
food.

Two round tablecloths, of different
lengths in contrasting fabrics, make a
feature of a plain table.
Fabric for a full-length cloth usually
has to be joined in three sections to
form a piece large enough to cut out the
circle, but by careful matching of the
pattern the seamline is inconspicuous.
Below: several ideas for table linen,
including a mat made of a single cut-
out motif, a quilted patchwork design
and examples of border edgings and
appliqué.

Table linen

MATS, NAPKINS, RECTANGULAR CLOTHS

There are no standard sizes for these. Your own needs, the width of the fabric being used, and its most efficient usage to avoid waste are the bases on which to decide dimensions.

Measuring and estimating

Napkins are usually square and may graduate from 30cm (12in) for tea size to 60cm (24in) for dinner size. However, with 90cm (36in) or 132cm (54in) width fabric, an all-purpose practical size is 40cm (16in) square so that the fabric can be divided evenly with enough for hem allowances and no wastage.

To estimate the fabric for one napkin, decide its finished size and add 10mm (½in) each side for hems (Fig. 1). For four 40cm (16in) napkins using 90cm (36in) fabric, or for six napkins using 132cm (54in) fabric, allow 90cm (1yd).

Tablemats. To decide the best size, lay the table with a standard setting of main and side plate, cutlery, glass etc. and measure the area used; add 5cm (2in) all round for a border and hem. An average size is 30 × 40cm (12 × 16in).

Tablecloths. If you have a cloth which fits the table, simply measure its width and length. Otherwise measure the length and width of the tabletop and, for a short cloth, sit in a chair and measure from the edge of the table to your lap; for a long cloth measure from the table to the floor (Fig. 2).

Add twice this measurement to each of the table top measurements. Add 5cm (2in) to each measurement for a narrow hem or 10cm (4in) for a wide hem. A hem allowance is not necessary for bound, frayed or zigzag stitched scalloped edges.

Fabric amount. Allow enough cloth to cut a rectangle with sides of the required dimensions.

Method

Cut out the fabric on the straight grain to the calculated size including any hem allowance. Make any joins necessary to form the fabric wide enough and finish the edges by one of the methods described in the Sewing Guide.

An alternative method for mats is to sandwich thin wadding between two layers of fabric. Cut the top fabric and wadding about 3cm (1in) smaller than the back, fold the backing forward with mitred corners (see Sewing Guide), and zigzag stitch over raw edges (Fig. 3).

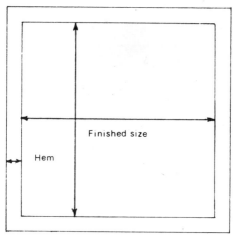

1. Estimating fabric for one napkin.

2. Measuring for a tablecloth. The length may be to your lap or to the floor.

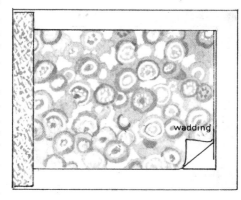

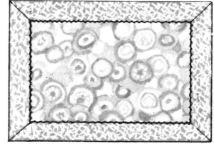

3. For a padded tablemat, sandwich thin wadding between two layers of fabric. Fold the backing fabric forward over the wadding and front fabric, after mitring and stitching the corners. Finish raw edges by zigzagging.

ROUND CLOTHS

Round cloths are normally used for dining tables or as permanent cloths on side tables. A floor-length cloth can be covered with a shorter version, as on page 16, and the shorter cloth can be either round or square. It can also be in a different colour, pattern or fabric (such as lace), or in a different texture, i.e. quilting.

Round cloths nearly always require joins in the fabric in order to get sufficient width. Always make joins on both sides of a central panel (Fig. 1) and keep side panels matching widths.

Measuring and estimating

Measure the diameter of the tabletop. Then for a short cloth, sit in a chair and measure from the table edge to your lap. For a long cloth measure from the table edge to the floor. Double the side measurement and add to diameter to get the total width. If you are finishing the edge with a narrow hem or stitching on a fringe, add 3cm (1in) to the diameter; for other finishes no hem allowance is needed.

Fabric amount. Allow enough fabric to cut a square with sides equal to the total diameter.

Method

Cut out a square of fabric on the straight grain of the calculated size, making any joins necessary. Fold the fabric in half lengthwise, then widthwise (Fig. 2), and mark the intersection of the folds with a tailor's tack.

Pattern. It is wise to make a paper pattern before cutting out the circle, but if you are confident then mark the fabric as described for the paper, but use tailor's chalk instead of a pencil.

Cut out a sheet of paper to the same size as the *folded* fabric.

Working on a flat surface into which you can insert a drawing pin (thumb tack), pin the paper in any corner to it (Fig. 3). Tie one end of a piece of string round the pin and tie the other end round a pencil, leaving half the total diameter, or radius, between them.

Holding the pencil upright, draw a quarter circle from B to C, then cut along the line. Place the paper pattern on the folded fabric with point A to the tailor's tack. Pin in position and cut along B–C (Fig. 4).

Remove the pattern and open out the fabric to form a complete circle. Finish the edge using one of the methods described in the Sewing Guide.

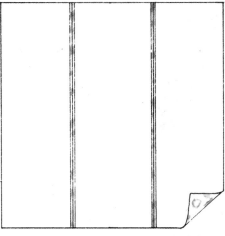

1a. To form fabric wide enough, join strips to sides of main panel.

1b. The position of the seamlines may fall across the table or at the sides.

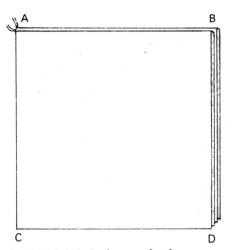

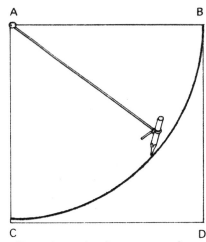

2. Fold fabric in four and take a tailor's tack at corner A.

3. To make a circular pattern, draw a quarter circle from B to C.

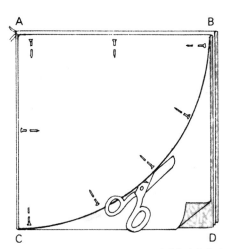

4. Place paper pattern on folded fabric so that point A is at the tailor's tack. Cut out along the curved line.

Sheets and duvets

RECTANGULAR SHEETS

The instructions given here are for plain hems. For alternative finishes such as hemstitching and binding, see the Sewing Guide.

Measuring and estimating

For measurements to fit a standard-size bed, see the chart overleaf. Measurements have been calculated on an average mattress depth of 10cm (4in) for cots and 15cm (6in) for other sizes. For non-standard sizes, measure (Fig. 1), and follow formula overleaf.

Fabric amount. Allow enough fabric to make a rectangle with sides of the required dimensions.

Method

Cut out the sheeting to length and trim off any excess width from one side, leaving 15mm (¾in) for a hem.

Make the hem by folding over 5mm (¼in) and then 10mm (½in) to the wrong side and machine stitching. There is no need for hems if the sides are selvedges.

For a plain hem at the top edge, fold 10mm (½in) to the wrong side and then 5cm (2in); machine stitch (Fig. 2).

For the bottom edge fold 10mm (½in) and then 3cm (1in) to the wrong side and machine stitch (see Fig. 2).

FITTED SHEETS

This style of sheet requires slightly less fabric than flat sheets because the fitted corners hold it in place.

Measuring and estimating

Add twice the mattress depth plus 20cm (8in) to the length and width of the mattress. Buy sheeting to these measurements and 1m (40in) of 15mm (½in) wide elastic.

Method

Measure the mattress depth plus 10cm (4in) along the edges from all the corners. Measure in the same amount on the straight grain at 90° to the edges, marking the lines with pins (Fig. 1).

Cut out a square piece 5mm (¼in) outside the pin lines and pin the cut edges of the sheet together, with right sides facing (Fig. 2).

Machine stitch, then neaten the edges together (Fig. 3).

Turn up a hem all round the edge, taking 5mm (¼in) with the first turning and 2cm (¾in) with the second. Machine stitch, leaving 2cm (¾in) spaces in the stitching for 15mm (6in) on each side of corner seam lines (Fig. 4).

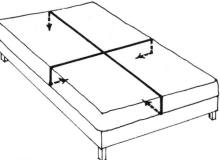

1. Measuring a bed for sheets.

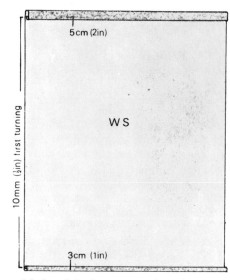

2. Make plain hems at each end.

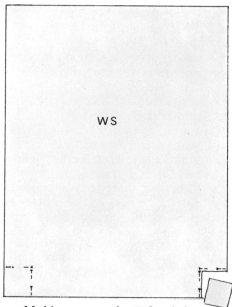

1. Making corners for a fitted sheet.

Cut the elastic into four pieces and thread one piece between the gaps through the hemline at each corner. Stitch the elastic ends in line with the openings (Fig. 5) so that the corners gather, and stitch up the openings.

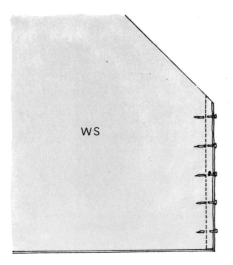

2. *Stitching corners together.*

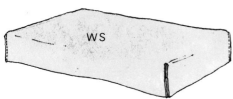

3. *All four corners stitched.*

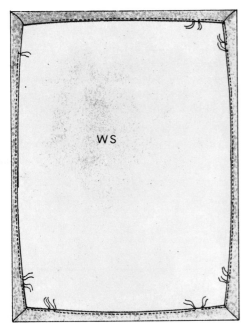

4. *Stitch hem, leaving gaps in stitching at corners for inserting elastic.*

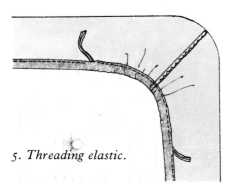

5. *Threading elastic.*

QUILT COVERS (DUVETS)

Continental quilts are becoming increasingly popular because of their lightness and the fact that they simplify bed-making. Continental quilt covers are made like a bag from one or two pieces of cloth, depending on the size of cloth available. To close the opening, use one of the methods described in the Sewing Guide or apply no-sew press-studs according to manufacturer's instructions.

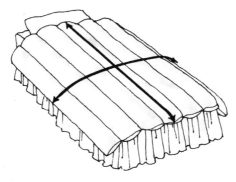

1. *Measuring duvet for a cover.*

Materials

Sheeting should be used to make continental quilt covers since unsightly joins will not be necessary.
A zip, press studs (mentioned above) or other fastening device is also needed.

Measuring and estimating

Check the dimensions of your quilt (duvet) (Fig. 1) – if they correspond with sizes on the chart overleaf, buy the amount of fabric shown; otherwise calculate the amount needed, using the formula overleaf. Choose the best formula for your own measurements and the width of fabric to be used.

Method

Cut out the cloth on the straight grain to the calculated sizes.
One-piece method. Fold the cloth in half, right side out, by placing the shorter edges together. Stitch each side from the fold to the opposite end in a french seam (Fig. 2), taking 1cm ($\frac{1}{2}$in) turnings (for french seams, see the Sewing Guide).
Make a hem round the opening, taking 5mm ($\frac{1}{4}$in) for the first turning and 1.5cm ($\frac{3}{4}$in) for the second (Fig. 3). Apply a fastening to the opening.
Two-piece method. Place pieces together with right side out. Stitch on three sides in a french seam with a hem round fourth side as one-piece method. Apply a fastening to the opening (Fig. 4).

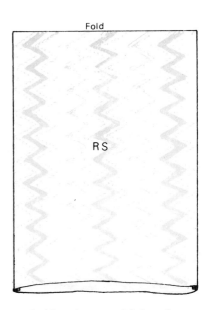

2. *Stitch sides of cover with french seams.*

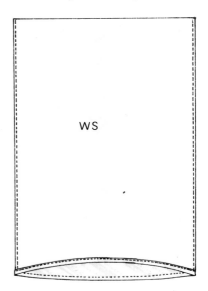

3. *Make a hem round the opening.*

4. *Duvet covers may be made from two pieces of fabric, if more convenient. Place pieces together and stitch with french seams on three sides.*

21

Measurement chart

Sheets		
Formula	Mattress length + twice depth + 10cm (4in) $\times$ Mattress width + twice depth + 4cm ($1\frac{1}{2}$in) if total does not match fabric width	
Size of bed	**Finished size**	**Fabric size**
Cot: 122 × 61cm (48 × 24in)	168 × 100cm (66 × 40in)	172 × 104cm (70 × 41$\frac{1}{2}$in)
Single: 190 × 75cm (75 × 30in)	254 × 135cm (100 × 54in)	264 × 139cm (104 × 55$\frac{1}{2}$in)
190 × 90cm (75 × 36in)	254 × 178cm (100 × 70in)	264 × 178cm (104 × 70in)
200 × 100cm (79 × 39in)	260 × 178cm (103 × 70in)	270 × 178cm (107 × 70in)
Double: 190 × 122cm (75 × 48in)	254 × 200cm (100 × 80in)	264 × 204cm (104 × 81$\frac{1}{2}$in)
200 × 135cm (79 × 54in)	260 × 230cm (103 × 90in)	270 × 230cm (107 × 90in)
200 × 150cm (79 × 59in)	200 × 230cm (103 × 90in)	270 × 230cm (107 × 90in)

Duvet covers		
Formula	a) Twice duvet length + 4cm ($1\frac{1}{2}$in) × duvet width + 4cm ($1\frac{1}{2}$in) b) Twice duvet width + 4cm ($1\frac{1}{2}$in) × duvet length + 4cm ($1\frac{1}{2}$in) c) Two pieces each of duvet length + 6cm (2in) × duvet width + 4cm ($1\frac{1}{2}$in)	
Size of bed	**Finished size**	**Fabric size**
Cot: 122 × 61cm (48 × 24in)	120 × 100cm (48 × 39in)	244 × 104cm (97$\frac{1}{2}$ × 40$\frac{1}{2}$in)
Single: 190 × 75cm (75 × 30in)	190 × 120cm (75 × 48in)	384 × 124cm (151$\frac{1}{2}$ × 52in)
190 × 90cm (75 × 36in)	190 × 137cm (75 × 54in)	384 × 141cm (151$\frac{1}{2}$ × 55$\frac{1}{2}$in)
200 × 100cm (79 × 39in)	200 × 150cm (79 × 60in)	404 × 154cm (159 × 61$\frac{1}{2}$in)
Double: 190 × 122cm (75 × 48in)	190 × 175cm (75 × 66in)	384 × 179cm (151$\frac{1}{2}$ × 67$\frac{1}{2}$in)
200 × 135cm (79 × 54in)	200 × 200cm (79 × 79in)	404 × 204cm (159 × 80$\frac{1}{2}$in)
200 × 150cm (79 × 59in)	229 × 218cm (90 × 86in)	562 × 222cm (181$\frac{1}{2}$ × 80$\frac{1}{2}$in)

Pillowcases	One-section method	Two-section method	
Formula	AC + 5cm (2in) × 2AB + 25cm (10in)	**bottom** AC + 4cm (1½in) × AB + 18cm (7in)	**top** AC + 4cm (1½in) × AB + 9cm (3½in)
Size of pillow 46 × 69cm 18 × 27in	51 × 163cm 20 × 64in	50 × 87cm 19½ × 34in	50 × 78cm 19½ × 30½in
50 × 75cm 20 × 29in	55 × 175cm 22 × 68in	54 × 93cm 21½ × 36in	54 × 84cm 21½ × 32½in
69 × 69cm 27 × 27in	74 × 163cm 29 × 64in	73 × 87cm 28½ × 34in	73 × 78cm 28½ × 30½in
40 × 58cm 16 × 23in	45 × 141cm 21 × 56in	44 × 76cm 17½ × 30in	44 × 67cm 17½ × 26½in

Pillowcases	Three-section method				Flat border method (pocket as for three-sections)	
Formula	**bottom** AC + 4cm (1½in) × AB + 4cm (1½in)	**top** AC + 4cm (1½in) × AB + 9cm (3½in)	**pocket** AC + 4cm (1½in) × AB + 16cm (6½in)	**frill** 1½ × 2AC + 2AB × 2 depth + 2cm (¾in)	**bottom** AC + 4cm (1½in) × AB + 5cm (2in)	**top** AC + 25cm (10in) × AB + 25cm (10in)
Size of pillow 49 × 69cm 18 × 27in	50 × 73cm 19½ × 28½in	50 × 78cm 19½ × 30½in	50 × 16cm 19½ × 6¼in	345cm 135in	50 × 74cm 19½ × 29in	71 × 94cm 24 × 33in
50 × 75cm 20 × 29in	54 × 79cm 21½ × 30½in	54 × 84cm 21½ × 32½in	50 × 16cm 21½ × 6¼in	375cm 147in	54 × 80cm 21½ × 31in	75 × 100cm 26 × 35in
69 × 69cm 27 × 27in	73 × 73cm 28½ × 28½in	73 × 78cm 28½ × 30½in	73 × 16cm 28½ × 6¼in	414cm 162in	73 × 74cm 28½ × 29in	94 × 94cm 33 × 33in
40 × 58cm 16 × 23in	44 × 62cm 17½ × 24½in	44 × 67cm 17½ × 26½in	44 × 16cm 17½ × 6¼in	294cm 117in	44 × 63cm 17½ × 25in	55 × 83cm 22 × 29in

Pillowcases

There are three main styles of pillow-case: plain (or housewife style), frilled (the frill may be matching or contrasting) and self-bordered (or Oxford style). The last two are made with a pocket inside the opening to hold the pillow without additional fastening but in the American version of the plain style the pocket is omitted.

Measuring and estimating
Start by measuring the dimensions of the pillow as shown in Fig. 1. If these correspond to a size on the chart on page 23, cut the fabric to that size. Otherwise calculate the amounts need-ed, using the formula. The amounts shown include turnings and ease.
American style. Use the fabric amount indicated for one-piece method but subtract 10cm (4in) from the width.

PLAIN PILLOWCASES

This is the simplest style to make and can be cut out in one, two or three sections, according to the fabric avail-able.

One-section method. Cut out on the straight grain, placing B–D to a selvedge, if possible (Fig. 2).
If B–D is not a selvedge, turn the edge in 3mm (⅛in) and zigzag stitch.
Make a hem across A–C, taking a first turning of 5mm (¼in) and a second turning of 5cm (2in). Machine stitch.
With wrong sides together, fold down B–D for 15cm (6in) and fold up A–C to meet the first fold so that the pocket is enclosed.
Stitch along the edges, taking 5mm (¼in) turnings. Trim to 3mm (⅛in).
Turn wrong side out and refold the pillowcase (Fig. 3). Stitch again, taking 5mm (¼in) turnings. Press.
Turn the pocket and the pillowcase right side out.
Two-section method. Cut out pieces and join raw long edge of pocket to main section using french seam (Fig. 4). Continue as for a one-section case.
Three-section method. Cut out pieces and join with french seam (Fig. 5). Continue as for a one-section case.
American style. Fold cloth in half, right side out, by placing the short edges together. Stitch each side from the fold to the opposite end, taking 5mm (¼in) turnings (Fig. 6). Trim to 3mm (⅛in).
Turn wrong side out and press so that seamlines lie along edges. Stitch from fold to opposite end taking 5mm (¼in) turnings.
Make a hem round the opening, taking a first turning of 5mm (¼in) and a second turning of 5cm (2in).

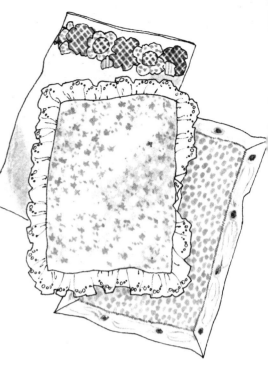

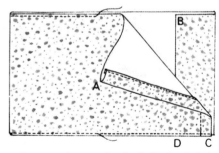

1. Measuring the pillow.

2. One-section method: fold the fabric as shown for a plain pillowcase.

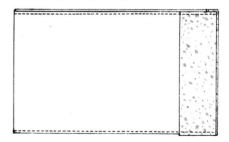

3. The one-section case, inside out, ready to complete the french seam.

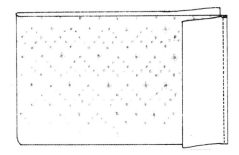

4. *Two-section method : the pocket is cut separately for convenience.*

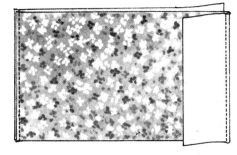

5. *Three-section method : the top, bottom and pocket are cut separately.*

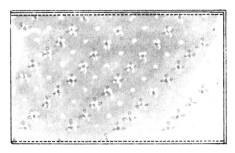

6. *American style : a plain case is made without an inside pocket.*

FRILLED PILLOWCASE

Frills can be made from bought trimming, such as *broderie anglaise*, or from fabric to match or contrast with the main part of the pillowcase. The width of the frill can vary according to personal taste.

To make a frill, join strips along short edges, then fold lengthwise, with wrong sides together, to eliminate a hem (Fig. 1) – treat layers as one.

Run a gathering thread all round the strip 5mm and 10mm ($\frac{1}{4}$in and $\frac{1}{2}$in) from the raw edge (Fig. 2).

Pull up the threads so that the frill fits the perimeter of the top section of the case and pin frill to its right side with raw edges together. Arrange the gathers evenly, placing slightly more fullness at corners. Baste.

Keeping the frill in the same position, continue as for a three-section plain pillowcase.

FLAT-BORDER PILLOWCASE

Cut out three sections following the directions in the measuring chart on page 23, and make a narrow hem along A–B, taking 5mm ($\frac{1}{4}$in) turnings. Fold edges of the top section (see Fig. 1) under 1cm ($\frac{1}{2}$in) and then 5cm (2in), and press.

Open out the second fold and mitre the corners (see Sewing Guide). Stitch mitred corners, right sides together, and refold them to form a border.

Make a narrow hem along one long edge of the pocket piece.

With wrong sides together, place the other raw edges of the pocket piece under the edge of the border; baste and zigzag stitch along X–Y only (Fig. 2).

With wrong sides together, place the bottom on the top so that the hem is at the pocket end. Keeping the layers flat, insert the raw edges evenly under the remaining sides of the top. Baste and zigzag stitch in position (Fig. 3).

A contrasting flat border like that on page 13 can be made as follows:

Decide depth of border and add 1.5cm ($\frac{1}{2}$in) turnings. Cut strips for border to twice this measurement × length of pillowcase sides.

Fold strips in half lengthwise, and mitre and stitch corners, right sides together.

Turn right side out and 'sandwich' border frame between main sections of three-section case. Proceed as for three-section method previously described.

Neaten inside raw edges with zig-zagging.

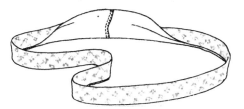

1. *Making a frill. It is folded in half to eliminate a hem.*

2. *Make two rows of stitches, then gather.*

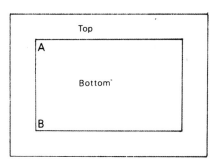

1. *Main pieces for a flat-bordered case.*

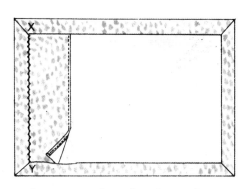

2. *Insert raw edges of pocket under turned edges of mitred border. Stitch along outside long edge only.*

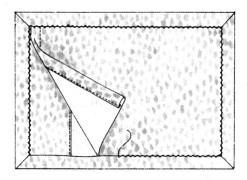

3. *Insert raw edges of bottom section under the mitred border. It is stitched through all layers.*

Bedspreads

THROW-OVER BEDSPREADS

This type of bedspread usually covers the bed completely and touches the floor at the sides and foot, although if a separate valance is fitted underneath the mattress, the bedspread could finish just below the top of the valance. The corners of the bedspread can be square or rounded (to avoid trailing)- and, instead of plain hems, the edges may be scalloped or finished with a fringe, frill, binding or reverse facing (see the Sewing Guide for details). Where the bedhead is against a wall or fitted with a board, the top edge of the bedspread is finished with a plain hem and the decorative finish applied to three sides only.

Joins. If using standard width fabric, you will almost certainly have to make joins to obtain the right width. The seamline can be disguised by trimming if desired. Position seams attractively by adjusting width of centre panel.

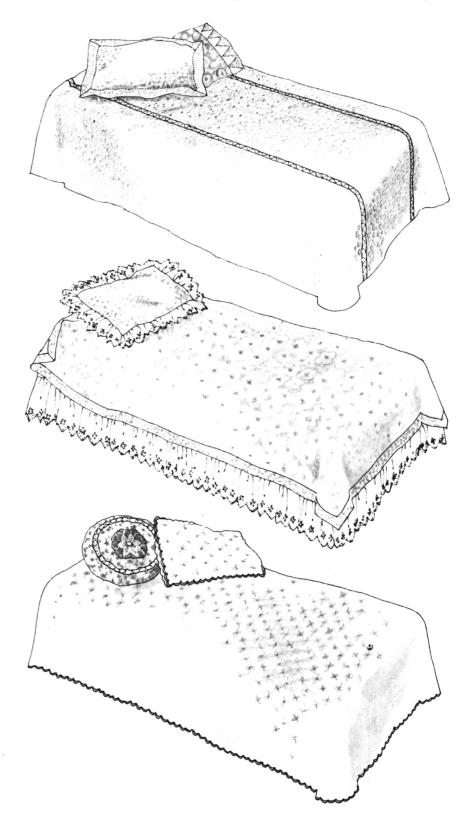

Measuring and estimating

Take measurements (Fig. 1) over usual bedclothes and pillows (unless decorative pillowcases are to be used on top of the spread). Remember to allow approximately 15cm (6in) to tuck beneath pillows.

Length. Measure from mattress to head, over pillows to desired length at foot.

Width. Measure from desired length on one side, across bed to same length on opposite side.

If fabric must be joined to make it wide enough, add 12cm (4in) to total width measurement.

Plain or scalloped hems. Add 6cm (2in) to each measurement.

Fringe or frill. Subtract length of frill or fringe from bedspread length and twice fringe or frill length from bedspread width. Add 4.5cm (1½in) turnings to length and 3cm (1in) to width. Calculate frill length as described in the Sewing Guide.

Binding. Add 3cm (1in) to bedspread length, nothing to width.

Facing. Add 4.5cm (1½in) to length and 3cm (1in) to width.

Method

If using more than one fabric width, cut the fabric widthwise to make pieces of the required length. If you now have two pieces, cut one in half lengthwise and join the halves along their selvedges to each side of the full piece, with right sides together, and taking 1.5cm (½in) turnings (Fig. 2); press turnings open. If using three full-width pieces, join them along their selvedges as for two pieces.

Trim an equal amount from each side, if required, for the correct width.

Plain hems, square corners. Make double hems all round, taking 1.5cm (½in) turnings and mitring corners; machine-stitch hems in position (Fig. 3). For information on mitring corners, see the Sewing Guide.

Plain hems, round corners. Measure required length of bedspread from top edge of mattress to the required overhang (A–B in Fig. 1) and add 6cm (2in).

Mark a square with sides of this length in each corner to be rounded (Fig. 4). Using a string and pencil with A–B as a radius, draw a quarter circle from B. Cut along this line.

Turn up a double hem all round the bedspread taking 3cm (1in) in each turning and notching the edge of the first turning to remove excess fullness (Fig. 5).

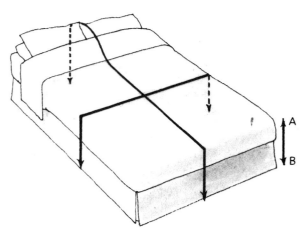

1. Measuring the bed. A-B length may vary if using bedspread over a valance or adding a frill.

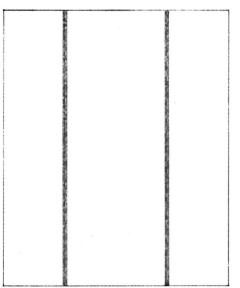

2. Join fabric.

3. Doubled hems, mitred corners.

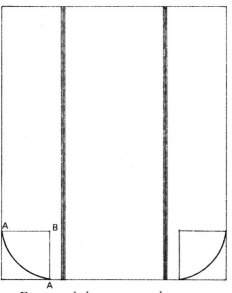

4. For rounded corners mark a square in corner, draw curve and trim excess.

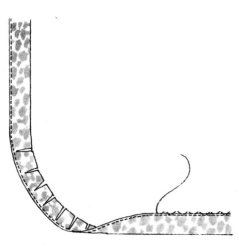

5. Finish edges with double hems; notch round curves to eliminate fullness.

FITTED BEDSPREAD AND VALANCE

A fitted bedspread and a bed valance (which is placed below the mattress to hide the bed base) are made in the same way, the main difference being the length of the skirt (you can economize with the valance by using a cheap fabric for the main panel, as this will not show). The skirt may be gathered, straight with inverted corner pleats or with pleats all round.

A more tailored style of bedspread can be made by inserting box strips (welts) of the same depth as the mattress between the main panel or top and skirt. All main seams may be piped.

Measuring and estimating

Take measurements over usual bed-clothes but without pillows as these distort the shape of the bedspread if they are placed under it (matching covers can be made for the pillows).

Take measurements as shown:

Main panel. Mattress length + 4cm (1½in) × mattress width + 3cm (1in). The main panel is the top surface of the bed.

Box strip. Mattress depth + 3cm (1in) × twice length + width of mattress + 8cm (3in).

Flounce. From top or bottom of mattress (according to style) to required length + 4cm (1½in) × three times length of mattress + one and one half times mattress width + 8cm (3in).

Tailored skirt. Two side strips of required length + 4cm (1½in) × mattress length + 20cm (8in); 1 bottom strip of same length × mattress width + 20cm (8in); 2 insert strips of same length × 18cm (7in).

Method

Cut out cloth on straight grain to correct measurements.

If the main panel was cut in sections, join them first as described for throw-over spreads.

Using a saucer or similar round object as a template, round off the bottom corners of the main panel to give a better fit and make the edge easier to sew (Fig. 1).

Box strip. Join short edges to make one strip. Mark centres of the long edges and match the centre of the top edge to the centre of the main-section bottom edge.

With right sides facing, stitch the two together, clipping the edge of the box strip round the curves to make a smooth line (Fig. 2).

Flounce. Stitch flounce pieces together right sides facing, and gather. Attach to the edge of the main panel or outer edge of box strip (Fig. 3).

Skirt. Turn up and stitch a hem on each strip, taking a 2.5cm (1in) allowance. With right sides together, and taking 1.5cm (½in) turnings, join the strips to form the following sequence: side strip, insert strip, bottom strip, insert strip, side strip (Fig. 4). Press turnings away from the inserts, then fold to form an inverted pleat. Baste in position (Fig. 5).

Matching the centre of the skirt top edge to the centre of the main-panel (or box strip) bottom edge, and with right sides facing, stitch the two together; clip the edge of the skirt round curves to make a smooth line.

Top edge. Trim the raw edge of the skirt, box strip and main panel level and form into a hem to finish the bedspread.

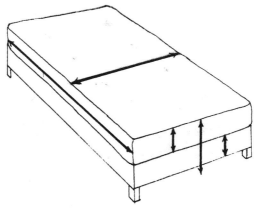

Measure bed as shown for a fitted bedspread or valance.

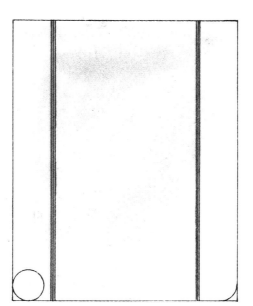

1. Round off corners of main panel, using a saucer as template.

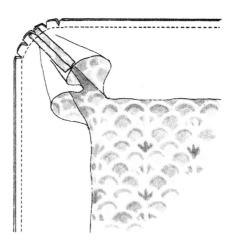

2. Attaching box strip (welt) to main panel. Clip edges at curves.

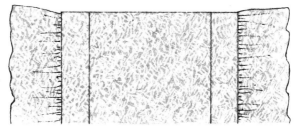

3. Attaching a gathered flounce.

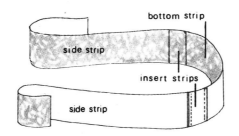

4. Joining the strips to make a tailored skirt with corner pleats.

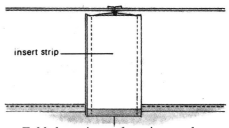

5. Fold the strips to form inverted pleats at corners of the bedspread.

Quilts

Quilting means sandwiching padding between two fabrics which are then stitched in an all-over pattern to hold the padding in place.

Originally, padding was made from whatever was available – tufts of sheep's wool, an old blanket, feathers from poultry and – most luxurious of all – goose or eider down. The work was placed on a large frame to keep the layers flat during the hand-stitching, which could take several months to complete. Inevitably intricate patterns developed, many of them symbolic, and quilting became a craft.

Modern materials and sewing machines have made quilting much speedier than it was a century ago when the craft was in its heyday. But even machine stitching traditional quilt patterns requires skill and time. *To make a quilt quickly*, use simple patterns based on straight or gently curving lines between 10 and 15cm (4in – 6in) apart (Fig. 1).

Fabrics

For the top layer choose cloth with a sheen which will show the quilting texture, such as satin or satinized cotton (sateen). Plain fabrics show stitching better than patterned ones although stitching can be worked round the motifs of the fabric design. The top layer can also be patchwork.

For the bottom layer use either the same type of fabric or sheeting, calico or a similar inexpensive cotton fabric. Buy the cloth to the finished dimensions of the quilt plus about 7.5cm (3in) all round to allow for turnings and the reduction in size that quilting makes. Buy the same amount of 1.5cm ($\frac{1}{2}$in) thick synthetic wadding for the middle layer.

Method

If making a large quilt, it will be easier to handle if worked in sections of about 50–60cm (20–30in). These can be joined later.

Plan the quilting design on paper, first deciding where the separate sections are to come so that the lines between them form part of the overall design.

Cut out cloth and wadding to size and draw or trace the quilting pattern in tailor's chalk on the top fabric, working from the centre outwards, and leaving the excess fabric unmarked.

Making. Lay the bottom fabric flat and place the wadding on it (Fig. 2), followed by the top layer, right side up. Baste edges and across the centre (Fig. 3). Repeat for each section. Work the quilting with a fairly long

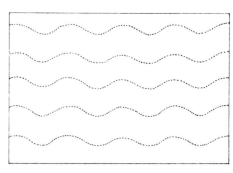

1. A simple quilting pattern which can be stitched by machine.

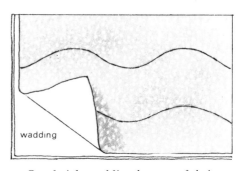

2. Sandwich wadding between fabrics.

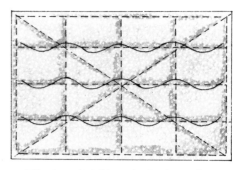

3. The 'sandwich' tacked, (basted) to hold layers together.

machine stitch, adjusting tension as necessary.

Joining sections. If working in sections, trim any excess fabric round the edges to within 1.5cm ($\frac{1}{2}$in) of the finished size. Fold the turnings on one section inside, trimming away the wadding so that it lies level with the folds (Fig. 4a). Trim the wadding from the adjacent section by a similar amount but do *not* fold the turnings (Fig. 4b). Instead, place them between the folded turnings of the first section, butting the wadding edges together, (see Fig. 5) and baste to within 2cm ($\frac{3}{4}$in) of folded edges and top-stitch through all layers. Repeat until all the sections are joined, to form long strips (Fig. 6) and then join the strips. Top stitch through all layers.

Finishing outer edges. Trim the wadding to the finished size and trim any excess fabric to within 1.5cm ($\frac{1}{2}$in) of it. Fold the turnings inside and top-stitch together.

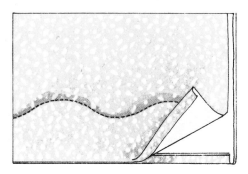

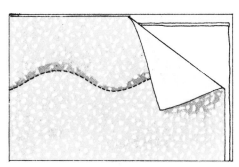

4a, b. Preparing to join sections.

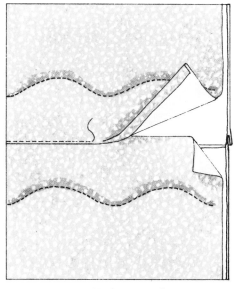

5. Joining the sections together.

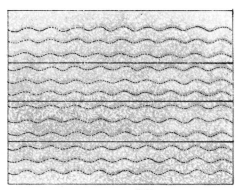

6. The sections are joined in long strips and then the strips are joined together as shown.

CONTINENTAL QUILTS

Continental quilts or duvets are much bulkier than stitched quilts and although they are often made in layers like stitched quilts, the stitching is widely spaced and functional, usually consisting of straight lines from head to foot.

Because the quilt has a removable cover (see page 21) the top and bottom are made from a plain fabric such as calico or sheeting.

Filling. The true continental quilt is filled with down or a mixture of down and feathers. The filling from an old eiderdown can be used but old filling will have become less efficient by one per cent a year (usually because of dust percolating through the cover).

If using an old eiderdown, additional filling will be needed, because duvets are fuller and larger than eiderdowns. A downproof cambric cover made with channels is also needed (this can usually be bought by mail order).

As an alternative to down and feathers, synthetic wadding is increasingly being used and it is probably the best type for making a duvet at home. It is less expensive than down and feathers, much easier to handle and is washable. Use sheeting or calico (muslin in USA) for the cover.

Measuring and estimating

A duvet should cover the bed and overhang the sides and foot by at least 23cm (9in) (Fig. 1) – see chart on page 22 for standard sizes. For children the overhang may be less.

Buy the special filling and two pieces of sheeting to the required size plus 3cm (1in) each way. If using calico (muslin USA), joins may be needed to make the width required.

Method

Cut out the fabric on the straight grain to size.

Using tailor's chalk, draw vertical lines about 23cm (9in) apart on the right side of one piece of sheeting. The lines should be equidistant.

Lay both sheeting pieces out flat with right sides together, then lay the padding on top (Fig. 2). Pin and stitch, taking 1.5cm ($\frac{1}{2}$in) turnings round three sides.

Turn right side out so that the padding is in the middle.

Fold in the turnings on the fourth side and top stitch (Fig. 3).

Using a long machine stitch (about five to 2.5cm (1in), stitch along the marked lines through all layers as shown in Fig. 4.

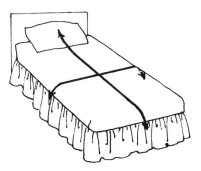

1. Measuring for a duvet.

2. Lay the wadding over the sheeting.

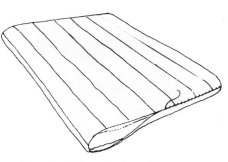

3. Topstitch the opening along the fourth side of duvet.

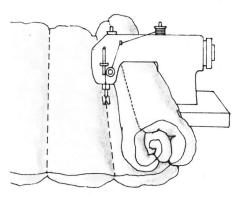

4. Machine stitch along length of duvet to hold wadding in place.

31

TRADITIONAL QUILTING

Quilting appears to have developed in China and was probably introduced into Europe from the Middle East by the Crusaders. Its original purpose was a means of keeping warm, but it also provided some protection in battle.

Quilting became immensely popular in 18th and 19th century America, even providing the focal point of a social occasion – the well-known sewing or quilting 'bee'. In both Europe and America traditional patterns developed, often using motifs drawn from nature – plants, shells – and from folk tradition – hearts. The technique was applied to a variety of bed covers: patchwork, appliqué, eiderdowns and, in America, there developed the most elegant showcase of all for the quilter's art – the white quilt stitched with white thread. The intricacy of design and fineness of stitch in some of these quilts class them among the greatest tributes to the craft of needlework.

Today, traditional quilting motifs like those shown here can be used on a variety of items and can be hand-stitched in running stitch (see the Sewing Guide) or machine stitched. Motifs can be used singly or as repeat patterns. Equally, the use of simple grid patterns can produce striking results, or a design motif on a piece of fabric which is outlined in stitching.

The objects shown on the opposite page illustrate some of the modern uses of quilting: basket linings, boxes, tea and egg cosies, slippers, sponge bags, oven gloves, hot water bottle cases, even curtains, can be embellished with quilting designs and at the same time serve the craft's original purpose of providing insulation.

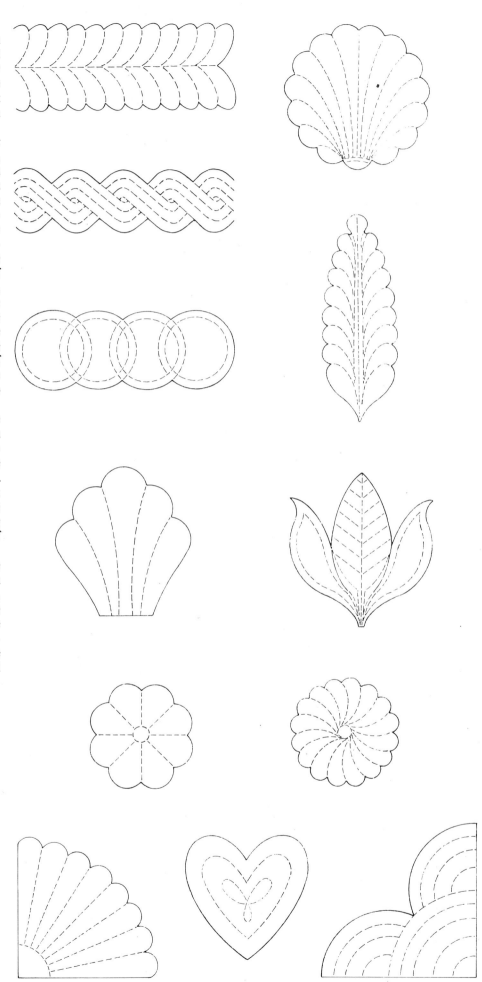

Cushions

The history of furniture has been chronicled since the ancient Chinese dynasties and the time of the pharaohs in Egypt, but cushions in some form or other were known to man much earlier and pads of fur, perhaps wrapped round straw or leaves, were probably the first 'furniture'.

Since then, cushions with various degrees of ornamentation have adorned chairs, thrones, settles and beds and have recently come into their own again as separate seating units.

Large floor cushions of plastic foam covered with heavy duty fabrics make substantial chairs, sofas or convertible beds, while small cushions, covered in printed fabrics or panels of needlepoint or embroidery, add a final decorative touch to a room.

Other useful positions for cushions are recessed window sills and benches: cushions can convert them from hard perches into comfortable seats.

The usefulness of firm cushions such as bolsters should not be overlooked. Bolsters make good improvised arm-rests and headrests on sofas and beds.

The arrangement of cushions is also important. An armchair often becomes more comfortable with one or two soft cushions in it, while sofas can sometimes benefit from masses of small cushions since these make a specially inviting spot to sink into. As a rule such cushions should be 'plumped up' and arranged regularly, but the arrangement should not look too formal or contrived as this would be at variance with the main principle of relaxation.

FABRICS

The fabric used to make cushion covers depends on the wear it will get and the overall effect desired. Almost any fabric, from heavy tapestry to fine cotton or lace, has its place.

Fitted, loose cushions on an upright chair, armchair or sofa, which get a lot of wear, should be made up in a fairly tough furnishing fabric such as velvet, corduroy, linen or union (a mixture of linen and cotton), or heavy cotton.

Synthetic fibres can also be used but, because of static electricity, they tend to pick up more dirt than do natural fibres. Cushions which are subject to less wear can be made up in lighter-weight dressmaking fabrics.

Fabrics for making up inner covers are described in the section on making up cushion pads.

Floor cushions epitomize relaxation.

Square and rectangular cushion covers

Measuring and estimating

The cushion cover should be the same size as (or slightly smaller than) the cushion pad to make plump, firm cushions, filled right to the corners. Use a tape measure to measure the pad to be covered. Add 3cm (1in) seam allowance to each measurement (Fig. 1). You will need two pieces this size. *Graph estimates.* If a number of covers are to be made from a fabric, it is useful to plan the layout first on graph paper.

First draw two parallel lines to represent the selvedges and then draw squares or rectangles to represent the fabric needed for the covers.

The example (Fig. 2) shows that two cushions 45cm (18in) square would need 1m of 120cm-wide (1¼yd of 48in) fabric.

If the fabric has a large pattern (Fig. 3), allow extra to centre the pattern.

Materials

Apart from the fabric and cushion pad the other materials needed depend on the way the cushion is to be fastened and on any trimming to be added.

Fastenings should be 10cm (4in) shorter than the length of the shortest edge of the cushion for plain or piped, unwelted cushions.

Piping cord and braid should be long enough to go round the cushion edges, plus an overlap of 3cm (1in). If the cushion is to be piped, you will need extra fabric, either the same as the main fabric or in a contrasting colour. For instructions on cutting bias piping strips, see the Sewing Guide.

Method

Lay the fabric on a large, flat surface and use a metre rule or yard stick and tailor's chalk to draw the cutting lines. Cut out the cushions carefully, following the grain of the fabric as far as possible.

Plain cover. Place the two pieces of fabric for the cover together, right sides facing and raw edges matching. Pin, tack (baste) and stitch round three sides, taking 1.5cm (½in) turnings. Neaten raw edges by overcasting or zigzag stitching.

Stitch about 5cm (2in) along each end of the fourth side. Clip corners (Fig. 4). Press the stitching along the seams. Turn back and press 1.5cm (½in) along the open edges.

Turn the cover right side out and put the cushion pad inside it, poking it right into the corners.

Slipstitch along open edge (see Sewing Guide).

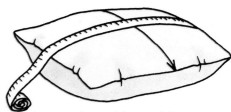

1. Measure the cushion pad from seam to seam, then add seam allowances.

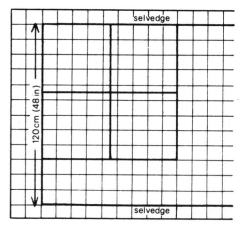

2. Plan a cutting layout on graph paper to estimate fabric requirements.

3. If fabric has a bold design or large pattern repeat, arrange each cover section centrally over a motif of the design.

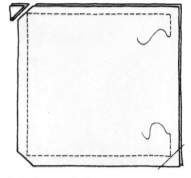

4. Stitch round the cover, leaving an opening to insert the pad. Clip corners.

Opposite : the decoration of cushions is even more varied than their shapes. Knitted or lace covers, inset panels, fabric paint, embroidery and appliqué are a few examples.

Plain cover with zip. Stitch 5cm (2in) along each end of one side of the cover, right sides together and raw edges matching (Fig. 5).

Insert a zip in the opening, making equal hems on each side (Fig. 6). (See Sewing Guide for details.) Press seam allowances round zip. Open zip slightly.

Turn cover so that the right sides of the pieces of fabric are together. Pin, tack (baste) and stitch the remaining three sides, matching the raw edges (Fig. 7). Press the stitching along the seams. Clip corners.

Turn the cover right side out and insert cushion pad.

Tape fastening. It is possible to use commercially produced tapes of press studs (snap fasteners) or hooks and eyes to fasten the opening. Proceed as for the plain cover, leaving an opening along the fourth side 10cm (4in) shorter than the length of the side.

Attach the fastening tapes to the right side of the seam allowance, on each side of the opening, ensuring that the fastenings match on each side. Clip the seam allowance at each end of one section of tape so that it will form an underlap and slipstitch the other section of tape to the wrong side of the cushion cover (Fig. 8).

Piped cushions. Make up the piping as directed in the Sewing Guide.

Pin, tack (baste) and stitch the piping to the right side of one of the cushion pieces, using the zipper foot or piping attachment of your sewing machine.

Piped cushions have to be made with slightly rounded corners to avoid puckering (Fig. 9), so position piping carefully at each corner. A flexible curve may prove useful here – bend it to the desired amount of curve and mark each corner by drawing round the curve with tailor's chalk. Alternatively, use a cup or saucer to mark the curve.

Neaten the ends of the piping (see the Sewing Guide).

Notch the seam allowance of the piping as shown. Continue as directed for covers without piping. If you are applying a zip, use the uneven hems method (see Sewing Guide).

Alternative zip application. If the cover has a definite 'right side' (e.g. needlepoint, a centred panel), or if the fabric is thick so that the seams (after piping) are too bulky to insert a zip easily, the zip may be inserted a short way from the seam.

For the back of the cover, cut two pieces of fabric. One piece should be the width of the cushion, plus seam allowances × 5cm (2in). The other piece should be the width of the cushion plus seam allowances the length of the cushion.

Pin, tack (baste) and stitch 6cm (2½in) at each end of the two pieces of fabric for the back of the cushion, right sides together and raw edges matching (Fig. 10).

Insert the zip in the opening, making even hems (Fig. 11). Press seam allowances round zip. Open the zip.

Place the two pieces for the cover right sides together, raw edges matching. Pin, tack (baste) and stitch round all four sides of the cushion.

Clip corners, neaten turnings and press along the seams. Turn the cushion cover right side out.

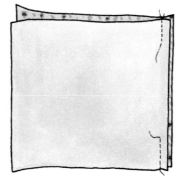

5. *Stitch 5cm (2in) at ends of opening.*

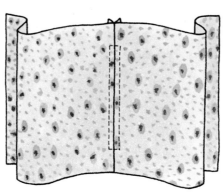

6. *Insert zip into opening.*

7. *Open zip and stitch round the remaining three sides. Clip corners.*

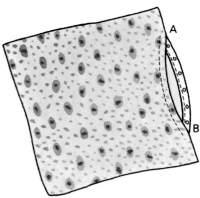

8. *An alternative fastening: apply press studs or hook and eye tape. Clip into seam allowance at A and B.*

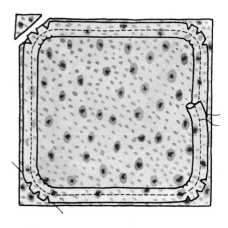

9. *Stitch piping to right side of one section, curving corners. Notch seam allowance of piping and clip corners.*

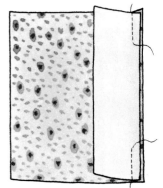

10. *Alternative zip application: stitch, leaving opening for zip.*

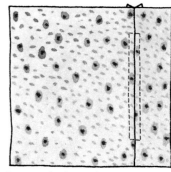

11. *Insert zip in opening.*

SQUARE, WELTED CUSHIONS

A welted cushion has a trim, firm appearance. A welt is the strip of material running round the cushion which forms the sides of the box shape. A zip or commercially pre-fabricated fastening tape is usually fitted in one of the welted sides. It is easier to insert the cushion if the opening extends 5cm (2in) round the adjoining sides.

Measuring and estimating

Measure the surface of the block to be covered and add 3cm (1in) to both dimensions for the seam allowances.

For the welt, measure round the block from the position of one end of the opening round the sides to the other end of the opening (Fig. 1). The depth of the welt is the depth of the cushion, plus 3cm (1in) for seam allowance all round.

For the back of the welt where the opening will be you need two strips of fabric the opening length × half the cushion depth. Add 1.5cm (½in) seam allowance to each end of strips.

If the seams are to be piped, add extra for cutting bias binding.

Method

Plain welted cushions. Join the strips for the welt, using flat seams. Press seams open (Fig. 2).

Fit the zip or strips of fastening tape between the two narrow sections of the welt (Fig. 3). (Stitch one of the seam allowances to the wrong side of the strip if using fastening tape, and press the other flat to form an underlap.) Join the ends of the section with the fastening to the main welt piece to make a length of welt which fits snugly round the cushion to be covered (Fig. 4).

Attach welt to lower cover section, right sides together, making neat square corners by pivoting the fabric on the needle of the sewing machine.

Clip into seam allowance of welt at each corner and clip across the corner of the seam allowance of the lower section (Fig. 5). Open the zip.

Repeat the process to attach the welt to the upper section. Press seam allowances towards the welt. Turn the cover right side out and insert cushion.

Piped, welted cushions. Make up the piping first. Two strips are needed, each the same length as the finished welt, plus an overlap of 2.5cm (1in).

Attach one strip of piping to the upper section (Fig. 6) and one to the lower section. Neaten the ends of the piping (see Sewing Guide).

Make up as described previously.

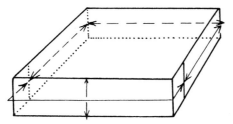

1. Measure round the sides of the block to estimate total length of welt.

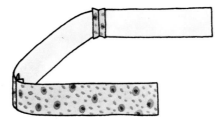

2. Join strips for welt, positioning seams inconspicuously.

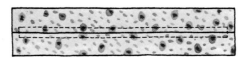

3. Apply zip between narrow sections.

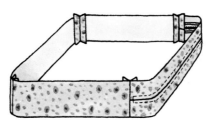

4. Join ends of zip sections to main piece and check for fit.

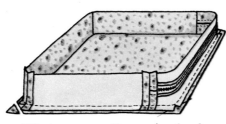

5. Clip into seam allowances of welt to make neat corners. Clip corners of lower section.

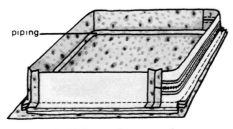

6. Attach piping to lower and upper sections before applying welt.

SOFA AND ARMCHAIR CUSHIONS

Cushions or cushion covers for sofas and armchairs are made in the same way as welted cushions and covers but they may have to be shaped slightly for a good fit. If the sofa or chair already has cushions, use these as templates to make paper patterns for the cushion covers.

Seat cushions are often slightly tapered towards the back. If this is the case, it is essential that the opening goes round the corners of the back section so that the cushion pad can be inserted easily.

Cut the fabric pieces to match the existing cushions, measuring the length of the welt carefully, adding 1.5cm (½in) seam allowances all round each section.

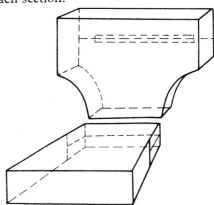

7. Shaped cushions for the seat and back of an armchair, showing positions for zips.

Back cushions may have indents to accommodate the arms of the chair or sofa (Fig. 7). Again, use the existing cushions as a template, and cut out pieces of fabric, allowing 1.5cm (½in) seam allowance all round.

If you do not have cushions, measure the chair or sofa carefully and draw the shape on paper. Dressmaker's graph paper is useful here. Cut out the appropriate shapes from paper and try them for fit on the chair or sofa before cutting out the fabric.

Make up the covers as directed for welted cushions. Position the opening on back cushions at the base of the cushion, with a good overlap round the side sections. The zip may be positioned down one side of the cover, at the seam, or right across the back of the cushion (Fig. 7). (Follow the instructions for the alternative method of inserting zips for round, welted cushions.)

Clip or notch the seam allowances and trim the corners as appropriate before turning the cover right side out. 39

PANELLED COVERS

A panel of fabric may be set into the cushion cover so that it is framed by the fabric from which the rest of the cover is made. The method is suitable for a wide range of panels, including needlepoint, lace, appliqué or reverse appliqué. A patch-work effect is possible by mounting one panel on another. Lace should be mounted on a piece of fabric *before* it is set into the panel frame – satin, silk crêpe de chine or miniature prints make effective backgrounds.

The panel is always set into the cover before the cover is made up.

Method

Measure the exact size of the panel to be framed, then allow a margin of 1.5cm ($\frac{1}{2}$in) all round.

Draw the rectangle on the right side of one section of the cover with tailor's chalk, centring the rectangle in the panel.

The panel may be positioned so that the sides are parallel to the sides of the cushion or the panel may be positioned diagonally.

Draw another line 1.5cm ($\frac{1}{2}$in) inside the first line to create a seam allowance. Cut out the shape, following this second line.

Snip diagonally into the corners of the seam allowance up to the corner of the original line (Fig. 1).

Turn the seam allowance under 1.5cm ($\frac{1}{2}$in) and press.

Position the panel under the hole and pin in place (Fig. 2).

Slipstitch the panel in place or, if the panel is not a hand-worked piece, tack and topstitch in place. Another alternative is to decorate the edges of the panel with zigzag stitch.

Mitred frame. The fabric frame may also be made with mitred corners (Fig. 3). (see Sewing Guide for instructions on mitring.) This is particularly suitable when using fabric with strong directional design.

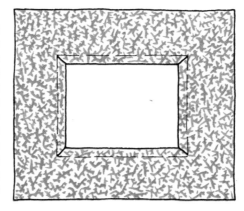

1. Cut out shape following inner line.

2. Pin panel behind frame and slipstitch.

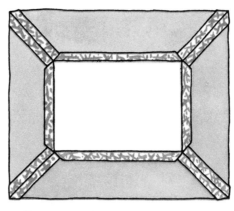

3. For a mitred frame, press open seam allowances, join corners and turn under inner edge, unpicking slightly at inner corners.

The large welted cushions in wicker chairs, opposite, are exactly like those normally used on sofas and armchairs. But in this case expensive upholstery has been dispensed with, although the comfort value remains the same. The small decorative cushions serve both to relieve the monotony of unbroken lines and to add to overall comfort.

Round covers

Round cushions can be disc-shaped, welted or cylindrical, but they are covered in much the same way as square cushions. The main problem with round cushion covers is ensuring that the fabric is perfectly circular.

Measuring and estimating

Measure the diameter of the cushions to be covered and add 3cm (1in) for seam allowance. For each side of the cushion, you will need a circle of fabric this size.

The opening for inserting the cushion on a slipstitched cover, or applying the fastening on a removable cover, should be about three-quarters of the diameter of the cushion, or one quarter of its circumference.

If the cushion is to be welted, you will need a strip of fabric the length of the circumference of the circle, less the length of the fastening, plus seam allowances × the depth of the cushion, plus seam allowances.

For the section of the welt where the fastening is to be attached, you will need two strips of fabric the length of the fastening, plus seam allowances × half the depth of the cushion, plus seam allowances.

Method

To ensure a perfect circle, cut a paper pattern first. Fold a square piece of paper, larger than the cushion, into quarters. Then, using string, a pencil and a drawing pin (thumb tack) so the distance from the drawing pin (thumb tack) to the pencil is the radius of the cushion, plus seam allowance, mark the perimeter as shown (Fig. 1).

Cut round the pencil line, open out the paper, and you will have a perfect paper pattern for cutting the main pieces of the cushion cover.

If the fabric has a strong design, centre the pattern over the centre of the design. Otherwise, use the pattern to cut circles from the fabric as economically as possible (Fig. 2).

Plain cushion cover. Pin, tack (baste) and stitch the two circular pieces together, with right sides facing, and raw edges matching. Leave an opening three-quarters of the length of the diameter (Fig. 3).

Press the stitching along the seams and turn under and press 1.5cm (½in) along unstitched section.

Notch seam allowances and turn the cover right side out. Insert the cushion pad and slipstitch the two sides of the opening together.

Piped covers. Cut the piping to the length of the circumference of the

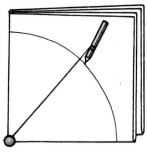

1. Draw a circular pattern, using string, pencil, drawing pin (thumb tack).

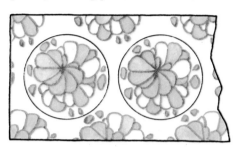

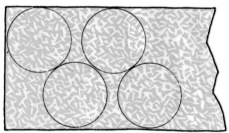

2. Plan cutting layout.

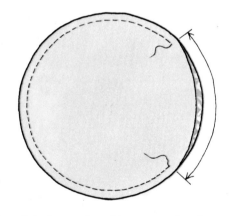

3. Stitch round cushion cover, leaving opening to insert pad.

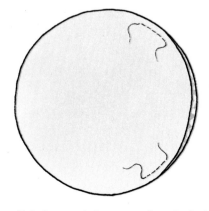

4. Stitch 5cm (2in) at each end of zip.

cushion, plus seam allowance. Attach the piping as for square cushions, to one side of the cover. Clip into the seam allowance of the piping so that it lies flat. Finish making up the cushion, preferably without a zip, as described above, notching the seam allowance of the piping as well as the cover.

Zips are best applied across the back of round cushions, unless they are welted, since zips in the side seams may cause puckering. All three methods are given here.

Plain cover with zip. Pin, tack (baste) and stitch 5cm (2in) at each end of the position of the zip, right sides together and raw edges matching (Fig. 4).

Turn cover right side out and insert zip in opening (Fig. 5).

Open the zip. Turn the cover inside out and pin, tack (baste) and stitch the remaining seam. Notch the seam allowances at intervals round the cushion (Fig. 6). (The smaller the cover, the closer the notches should be.)

Alternative method of inserting zip. The zip may be inserted straight across the back of the cushion.

After cutting the front of the cover, divide the paper pattern so that you have a line across the pattern 13cm (5in) longer than the length of the zip. Cut the pattern along this line (Fig. 7). Cut out two sections for the back of the cover but, before you begin, move the two pattern pieces apart 3cm (1 in). This creates the seam allowance for the zip.

Cut out the cloth as shown in Fig. 8 so that the circle is perfect but the zip seam allowance is included.

Join the two pieces together (right sides together and raw edges matching) for 6.5cm (2½in) at each end of the zip seam allowance (Fig. 9).

Insert a zip in the opening, making equal hems (Fig. 10).

Continue to make up the cover sewing right round the main seam and leaving the zip partially open while you are making the cover, so that you can turn the cover right side out when it is completed (Fig. 11).

Round, welted covers. Insert the zip between the two narrow sections of the welt and join the sections of the welt with flat seams, as described for square welted cushion covers (Fig. 12). Check for fit.

Attach piping to each of the circular sections of the cover, if wished, then attach welt but notch welt seam allowances *before* stitching together, then press towards the welt (Fig. 13).

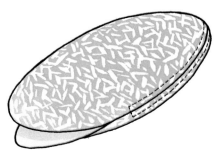

5. Insert zip in opening.

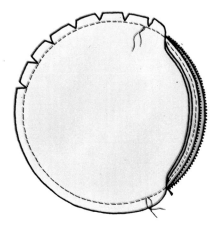

6. Stitch remainder of seam round cover. Notch seam allowance.

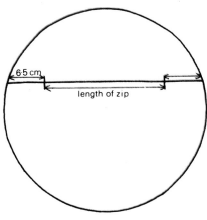

6·5 cm

length of zip

7. Mark a seamline across the paper pattern longer than the zip.

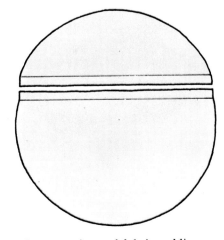

8. Cut two pieces of fabric, adding seam allowance along each side as shown.

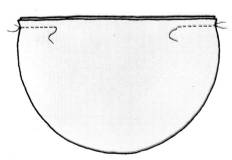

9. Stitch short section at each end.

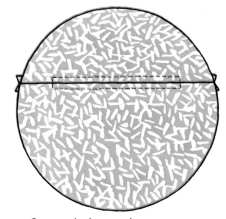

10. Insert zip in opening.

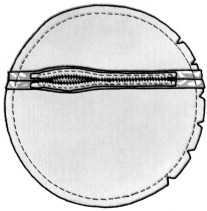

11. Stitch round cushion. Notch seam.

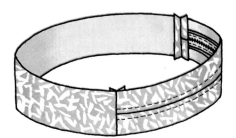

12. Zip application on welted cushion.

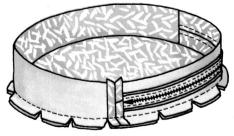

13. Attach welt to right side of one circular cushion section. Notch seam. 43

BOLSTERS

These long, firm cushions were traditionally used as under pillows on beds or as firm cushions at the ends of couches.

Measuring and estimating

Measure the length of the bolster and its circumference. The main piece for the bolster must be this size, plus 3cm (1in) in length and width for seam allowances.

For the end pieces, two circles of fabric the same diameter as the bolster, plus 1.5cm (½in) all round are needed. Make a pattern for the circular ends of the bolster as described for round cushions.

The zip for the bolster must be at least half the circumference of the bolster, so that the cushion pad can be inserted easily.

Method

Pin, tack (baste) and stitch the two edges which are the length of the bolster, right sides together, leaving an opening in the centre of the seam for applying the zip (Fig. 1).

Apply the zip in the opening, with even hems on each side (Fig. 2).

Open the zip and turn the tube inside out. Pin, tack (baste) and stitch the circles to each end of the tube, clipping turnings on tube *first*, and applying piping if wished.

Notch the seam allowances of the turnings (Fig. 3) and press towards the circles of fabric.

Turn the cover right side out and insert the cushion pad.

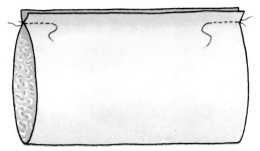

1. Stitch seam, leaving an opening.

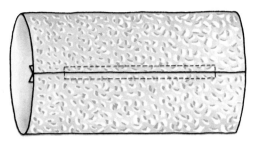

2. Insert zip in opening, making equal hems on each side of the zip.

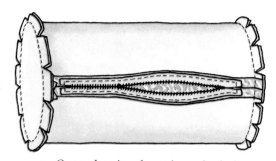

3. Open the zip, then pin and stitch the circular sections to each end of the tube, right sides facing. Notch seam allowances.

ROUND PANELLED COVERS

Round panels may be mounted on a circular (or square) cushion in much the same way as rectangular panels (described on page 40). The same materials may also be used.

Method

Measure the diameter of the piece to be framed, leaving a 1.5cm (½in) margin all round. Use a compass or string and pencil as described earlier to mark a circle the necessary size on the front of the cover. Make another circle 1.5cm (½in) inside the first.

Cut out a circle of fabric, following the line of the inner circle.

Clip the seam allowance round the inner circle, up to the original replacement lines (Fig. 1), and press under.

Pin panel in position under hole and, working right side up, slipstitch panel to frame (Fig. 2).

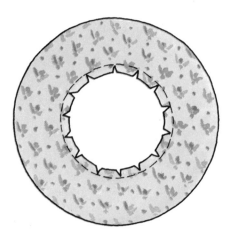

1. For a round, panelled cover, cut out frame section, clip into seam allowance, turn under and press.

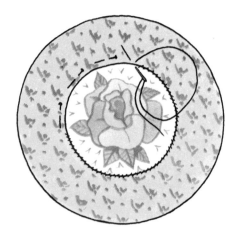

2. Pin decorative panel in position under cushion cover frame and slipstitch the panel neatly in place.

44

Lace cushions produce a decidedly feminine ambience. Lace can be applied to the front of a cushion, made up as a case, or inserted into a central panel. In all of these a backing fabric must be used both to strengthen the cover and to provide a background for the delicate tracery of the lace. Backing fabrics can be softly coloured silk or satin, or tiny cotton prints like those shown here.

Cushion pads

Cushion casing can be made from calico, ticking, cambric, lining material, old cotton sheets. However, if the cushion is to be stuffed with feathers and/or down, it is essential to have down-proof ticking for the casing.

Method

Decide the size you want the cushion to be and cut the size plus 1.5cm (½in) for turnings.

Make the casing in the same way as the cushion cover previously described, but omit any piping, trimmings or fastenings.

If the cushion is to be stuffed with feathers or down, the seams should be machine stitched with a fine needle, and stitched twice. Otherwise make french seams.

Leave an opening of about 15cm (6in) along one side of the cushion pad before clipping the corners and turning the pad right side out.

Stuffing

Foam chips are probably the cheapest form of stuffing. They are not absorbent so they are particularly suitable for making nursery cushions or cushions which are to be used outside. They must be very firmly packed into the cushions as they tend to look lumpy.

Acrylic and polyester wadding have similar properties to foam chips, but are less lumpy and more expensive. They have the added advantage of being completely washable.

Kapok. A more traditional stuffing is kapok, a vegetable fibre. Kapok is also non-absorbent but it does tend to go lumpy after a few years and is a little more expensive than man-made fillings.

Feathers are considerably more expensive, but make lovely, soft cushions which can be plumped up again and again.

Down is the softest and most expensive filling, and for this reason it is often used in combination with feathers. Down tends to plump itself up.

Foam. For square or circular welted cushions, plastic or latex foam in a block is useful as it does not lose its shape.

Do not be tempted to omit the casing as the blocks begin to crumble after some years, so that crumbs of foam collect inside the cover. When the block loses its 'give' and starts to deteriorate, throw out the complete inner cover and foam block and replace it.

Note. A cushion 45–50cm (18in–20in) square takes about 800g (1½lb) foam chips, 700g (1¼lb) synthetic fibre chips, 700g (1¼lb) synthetic fibre or kapok, 900g (2lb) feathers, or 350g (¾lb) down.

Stuffing cushions can be a messy business, so do it outside if possible.

If you are stuffing a new casing with the filling from an old cover, this can be done by joining the two cushions. Leave a 15cm (6in) opening in the new cushion cover. Unpick one seam of the old cover for 15cm (6in). Tack the two cushion covers together round the openings, and ease the stuffing out of the old cover and into the new one (Fig. 1). Unpick the tacking and slip-stitch the open edges of the new cover together.

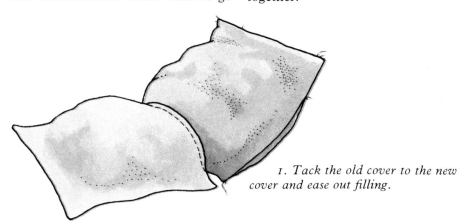

1. Tack the old cover to the new cover and ease out filling.

Whether cushions are round or square, welted or bolsters, they invariably serve the dual purpose of giving comfort and being decorative.
Opposite are just a few examples of pretty possibilities.

Lampshades

Lampshades are important accessories in every furnishing scheme and, although essentially functional, they are also decorative, both in appearance and in the effects of the light dispensed.

The choice of shade is probably secondary to the choice of base, but there are nevertheless many very important factors to be considered. Obviously the style must blend with the decor in the room. Contemporary rooms often need lampshades of bold design and colour, while gently contoured shades in pale colours are more in keeping with traditional surroundings.

It is important to bear in mind that light can be affected by the colour and texture of the lampshade. If it is translucent, pale pink, peach or cream colours produce a soft rosy glow. Silk and parchment are traditionally useful to this end but cotton can produce a similar effect.

Translucent white, red and orange are generally too glaring and tiresome to sit with for long and blues tend to produce a cold, hard glare. If there is doubt over colour or covering materials, it is well worth experimenting with scraps of fabric held over a lit but unshaded lamp, for the effect. It can also be observed how much or how little light is radiated through the shade. Very dark colours or opaque card will, of course, block out light entirely except where the beams shine above and below the cylinder of the shade.

The entire colour scheme of any room becomes totally changed with night lighting and the effects caused by different shade colours and textures can be quite dramatic. Here again the purpose of the shade matters. Lamps intended for reading must be shaded with a suitably light colour, especially bedside lights. Darker, plain colours and prints can give a restful, even romantic, atmosphere.

Proportions. In choosing a lampshade frame it is very important to get the proportions of base and shade correct. These can vary a great deal according to personal taste but as a safe, general rule the shade should be much the same height as the lamp base and the diameter of the bottom of the finished shade should equal the height of the lamp base. Careful thought must be given to selection, to avoid ending up with a fine shade that looks ridiculously large or small for its base.

Materials. Lampshades can be made from a number of different materials and, when choosing material, it is important to keep in mind the intended use and position of the lamp.

The degree of translucency is of course, the first consideration. Fabrics which produce translucency – silk and some cottons – must be lined, and this should be taken into consideration when gauging the amount of light which will penetrate through the finished shade. (Part of the purpose of the lining is, in fact, to *reflect* light, not to filter it.)

As has been stated, parchment, the traditional material for lampshades, produces a warm, translucent glow. True parchment is made from animal skins and nowadays is both rare and expensive, but a number of special papers are available – though not very widely – which produce similar effects.

As a rule, although paper or card shades tend to be opaque they can still produce considerable light. The lampshade opposite, for example, radiates a wide circle of light at the bottom, while the top opening is much smaller, thereby increasing the reflective powers of the inside of the shade.

Paper and card are very popular for use in contemporary decors because of their crisp, clean lines. However, the papers available are limited both in hues and in printed designs. Wallpaper can be used for lampshades but a backing is usually needed to stiffen it. Wallpaper should never be used too close to the bulb.

It is also possible to make a stiff fabric-covered shade by dampening the shiny side of buckram and ironing fabric on. Some craft shops sell special iron-on backing for this purpose.

Innovations. In this chapter the traditional methods of making fabric and paper lampshades are treated in detail, but even simpler versions are possible. Essentially lampshades are means of masking glare or reducing intensive light and, while established modes of doing this have developed over the years, there is always room for improvisations such as the 'handkerchief' shades overleaf or the fabric circle on page 60. So, before you begin, it is well worth having a think about easy new styles as well as known ones.

The lampshade on the right has a conical or 'coolie' shape which throws most of the light downward in a broad circle. Because of this wide pool of light, such lamps are particularly useful for chair-side reading lamps.

HANDKERCHIEF LAMPSHADES

These are probably the simplest of all lampshades. They make attractive decorations in a child's room or other room where informality is a keynote.

Materials

All that is needed is a utility ring (see overleaf), or a metal 'coolie' shade of the same shape, and a square metre (yard) of fabric.

Method

Hem the fabric square with a narrow double hem turned to the wrong side, or use a zigzag stitch as shown here (in which case, cut the outer edge *after* the border has been stitched).

Find the centre of the fabric by folding it in four and marking with tailor's tack. Then cut a hole just large enough to string the electric wire or chain through. Either bind this with overcasting or zigzagging.

Run the cord or chain through the hole and attach or connect the fixture.

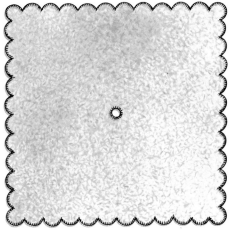

Handkerchief lampshades involve lampshade-making at its simplest, yet the result is full of charm.

51

TYPES OF FRAME

There are two groups of frames: those with side struts, suitable for fabric coverings, and those with separate rings in various sizes which can be easily adapted to make many different sizes and shapes of shade. Within each of the two groups of frames mentioned, there are fittings for standard (floor), table, clip-on, and hanging shades.

PREPARING FRAMES

Lampshade frames are either made of plastic-coated metal or copper wire. The shapes which are normally available are shown opposite.

To ensure a firm, sound foundation for the shade, some preliminary work may be necessary on the frame.

Copper wire frames. Examine the frame thoroughly. File down any rough or sharp areas at the joints of struts to prevent possible damage later to binding tape or covering.

If the finished shade is likely to be washed, risk of rusting can be reduced considerably by painting the frame with plastic varnish or gloss paint.

The frame may be a little out of alignment; if so, correct the shape and straighten any bent wires.

Plastic-coated frames. These should need little preparatory work apart from wiping free from dust, but in some cases the plastic may have been applied rather thickly, leaving a bump. Carefully smooth this by shaving off excess plastic with a sharp knife. Most table lamp frames have a tilting gimbal, but its hinges are often rendered immobile by the plastic-coating process. With a sharp knife simply cut through the plastic to the hinges on each side of the gimbal. Then the frame will tilt freely to a desired angle.

Re-using old frames. Recovering old frames may be from choice or necessity. It is sometimes possible to buy old, unwanted or worn out shades, but with perfectly sound frames. Some old fashioned shapes are quite lovely and well worth searching for. Also lack of availability of new lampshade frames may compel the recovering of existing frames.

All covering, trimmings and binding tape must be removed from an old frame, stripping it bare to the wires.

Rub off every apparent scrap of rust with fine sandpaper and wipe off all loose rust very thoroughly.

Correct the shape, if distorted, and paint or varnish frame as recommended for new copper wire frames.

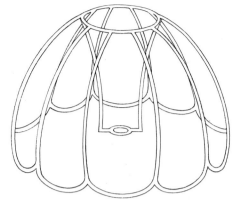

Tiffany

Butterfly clip for small shades

Pendant fitting on tiffany shade

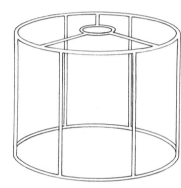

Straight-sided drum

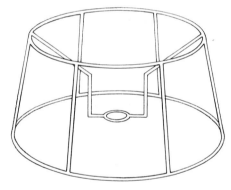

Tapered drum

Bowed drum

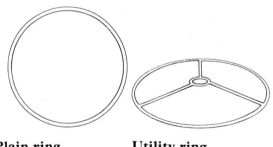

Plain ring   **Utility ring**

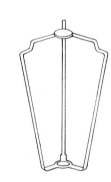

Duplex shade support

Gimbal rings

Duplex ring

TAPING FRAMES

For fabric shades and most shades made of rigid materials, it is necessary to bind the metal frame to provide a firm base on which to stitch the cover. Both the lining and the cover of fabric shades are attached to the top and bottom rings of the frame by stitching them to the tape on the rings. Paper is glued to the taped rings, then stitched.

Type of tape. Soft, straight, woven cotton tape is the most suitable for binding. If obtainable, use a loosely woven, inexpensive quality made specially for the purpose. It is 13mm (½in) wide and can be easily dyed to match the lining or the cover.

Bias binding may also be used, its advantage being that it is available in a wide range of colours. Bias binding tends to produce a bulky finish, but that can be reduced by ironing one folded edge open before using.

Estimating tape. Measure round the circumferences of rings and lengths of the vertical struts, then double the total measurement. Do not include the actual light fitting wires, or gimbals, or pendant wires in the measurements as these must never be bound with tape.

Binding

This is made easier if the tape needed for each section is wound into a bundle and secured with a rubber band; then a little at a time can be released without becoming twisted or tangled.

First tape each strut separately, always starting and finishing where the strut joins a top or bottom ring.

Fold one end of tape under the top ring and down the outside of the strut for about 25mm (1in) as in Fig. 1.

Wind the bundle of tape round the strut, covering the starting end, and bind diagonally to the bottom. Overlap each round of tape about 3mm (⅛in) over the previous round.

The tape must be wound very smoothly to avoid unsightly ridges and very tightly to avoid any possibility whatever of slipping. If this should happen, the cover will be slack and baggy instead of being taut and the shade will be spoiled before it is really begun. If the tape is loose enough to twist on the wire, then it must be undone and properly wound. When the lower end of the strut is reached, wind the tape over the outside of the lower ring to the back. Then pass the end of the tape through the loop to form a half knot (Fig. 2). Pull the knot tight. Tape all but one of the remaining struts in this way.

Tape the top ring next, starting at the upper end of the untaped strut. Place the end of the tape along the outside of the ring and take the rest of the tape round the ring and over the strut (Fig. 3).

Wind all round the top ring. Make a figure-of-eight round the top of each strut as it is reached (Figs. 4 and 5). When the top ring is completely taped, work down the remaining strut and round the bottom ring. Again work a figure-of-eight round each strut as it is reached.

To finish, fold under about 6mm (¼in) of tape end and stitch neatly to outside of bound ring.

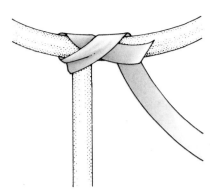

3. Tape the top ring, beginning at an untaped strut.

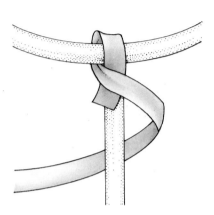

1. Fold one end of the tape under the top ring and up over it, as shown.

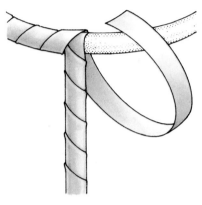

4. Wrap the tape round the top ring until another strut is reached.

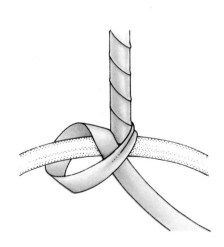

2. Forming a knot to secure the tape at bottom of strut.

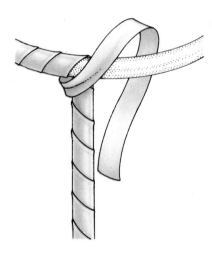

5. Make a figure of eight round each strut as the top ring is taped.

53

Fabric covered lampshades

A wide variety of furnishing and dress fabrics can be used for lampshades but fabrics with a certain amount of 'give' are the best and the easiest to work with; they are less likely to wrinkle when stretched over the frame.

Linings are used to conceal the struts and framework and to reflect light from inside the shade. It is therefore more sensible to choose a pale fabric, and one that is light-weight but strong. Crêpe back satin is particularly good for lining, the shine gives a warm and pleasant glow. However, cotton lawn, soft fine poplin and taffeta are also recommended. A white lining will reflect maximum light, but cream, ivory and pale, peachy colours throw out a softer, warmer light.

Materials

You will need binding tape, good steel pins and fine, sharp needles, sewing cotton, tape measure plus the cover and lining materials and trimmings.

TAILORED COVERS WITH BALLOON LININGS

Not only is this the most useful basic method of lampshade making, it is, once understood, the most straight-forward. Both the covering and lining fabrics are prepared in the same way and can be applied to most curving or straight strutted empire, oval and drum frames. First, the cover is stitched to the taped frame and then the lining is inserted.

Measuring and estimating

Allow fabric to cut a rectangle with width equal to the circumference of the largest part of the frame plus 15cm (6in) and length equal to the depth of the frame plus 75mm (3in).

Note: if the rectangle is wider than fabric, cut two rectangles, each of half required width.

For waisted shades, rectangle should be on *bias grain* to give greater flexibility. For other shapes it should be on the *straight grain*.

The same amount is needed for lining.

Method

To prepare the outer cover, fold fabric in half lengthwise, with right sides facing and tack (baste) cut edges together to stop the fabric slipping. Place doubled fabric to half the frame, with fold to one side, so that the straight grain of fabric runs up and down the shade (Fig. 1).

To do this, first pin to each side strut, working the fullness outwards to the sides; then pin fabric to top and bottom rings (Fig. 2), tightening fabric where necessary to eliminate all wrinkles and ensure a tight close-fitting cover. Always pin inwards.

On straight drums, tighten fabric from top to bottom rings first, before pinning to side struts, to keep a true shape. *On waisted shades,* tighten fabric diagonally to avoid distorting the grain.

When pinning is completed, mark a faint line of pencil dots down each side strut between the pins to mark the seam line (Fig. 2).

Remove cover from frame and baste, and stitch down along the pencil lines. Trim seams to 6mm ($\frac{1}{4}$in) (Fig. 3).

Press the work carefully so that the double seam allowance is to one side: do not press the seams open. Turn work right side out.

Prepare the lining in the same way as the cover but stitch seams 3mm ($\frac{1}{8}$in) inside pencil lines. Put aside.

Fitting outer cover. Slip the cover over the frame, making sure that the side seams run down the side struts, with the seam allowance actually behind the strut. It will not then be too obvious when light is behind it.

Pin top and bottom edges in turn to upper and lower rings. It is very important at this stage that the side seams do not slip out of position.

Using double cotton thread, oversew both ends of the cover to the tape on the frame (Fig. 4). Use small stitches through the fabric to the outer edge of binding tape.

Trim off surplus fabric from top and bottom edges, as close to the stitching as possible (Fig. 5).

Insert the lining into the shade, matching seams exactly with those of the cover and with the right side showing on the inside.

Pin the lining to top and bottom rings, as shown in Fig. 6, adjusting where necessary to make fabric taut and smooth.

Slit the fabric to fit it neatly round each arm of the gimbal.

Oversew all round, making sure the stitches are on the outer edge of the shade so that the trim will cover them completely. Trim off excess fabric.

Gimbal. Now neaten the area round the gimbal fitting wires. Cut a strip of the lining fabric 75mm (3in) long and 25mm (1in) wide, fold into three lengthwise and press.

Pass the strip under the gimbal fitting, raw edges hidden underneath (Fig. 7). Bring ends of strip together, fold over ring and stitch to outside edge of ring. Repeat for other fitting wire. Apply trimming described on page 63.

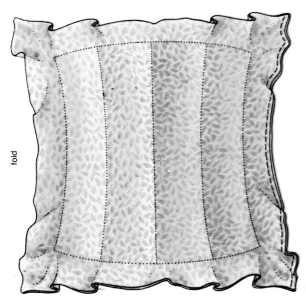

fold

1. *Place doubled fabric over half of frame.*

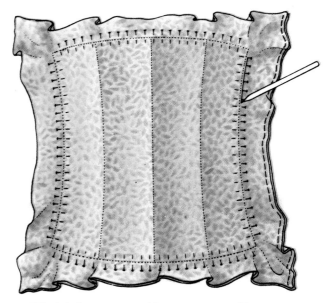

2. *Pin fabric to tape on side struts, top and bottom.*

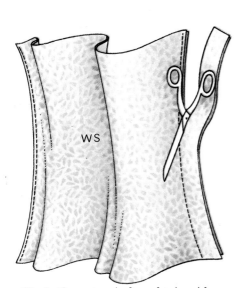

WS

3. *Tack (baste), stitch and trim sides.*

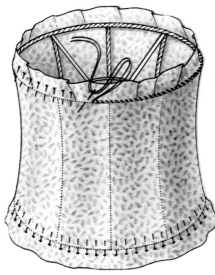

4. *Oversew both ends of cover to tape.*

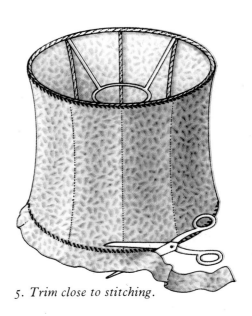

5. *Trim close to stitching.*

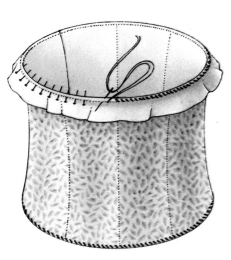

6. *Attach lining to top and bottom rings.*

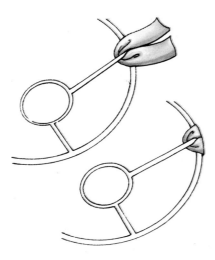

7a and b. *Neaten gimbal fitting.*

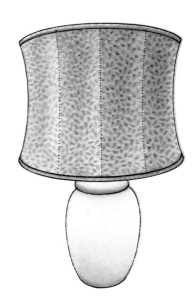

PLEATED COVERS

Covering fabrics for these shades must be soft and light; silk chiffons, georgettes and light cottons are recommended. Strutted frames are used and the frame must be taped as described earlier.

The lining is prepared as for tailored shades, but it is inserted and fixed before the cover. This gives a firm foundation on which to stitch the pleats.

STRAIGHT PLEATED DRUM
Measuring and estimating

For the length of fabric allow 2½-3 times the circumference: for the width, add a bit extra to the depth of shade.

Method

Insert lining.
Turn one short end of the fabric under 6mm (¼in) and pin to tape on one strut. The grain must be straight.
Pleat along one edge of the fabric and pin to one ring (Fig. 1). Each pleat must be the same width and all fold lines must be straight with the grain. When the second strut is reached, pleat the other end of the pleated fabric to the other ring and pin in position. Continue working round the frame, to one strut on the bottom ring, then as far as the same strut on the top ring. There must be the same number of pleats between each strut.

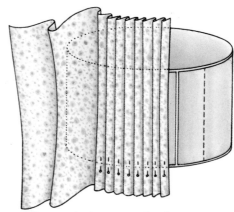

1. Pleat and pin to one ring between two struts, then pleat and pin other end.

Any joins in the fabric are not stitched, the edge of the new length of fabric is simply turned under the width of the pleat to become part of the pleat. The last end of the fabric is folded under to make a pleat in the same way.

When pinning is completed, oversew all round pleats to both rings and trim off surplus fabric as for outer cover of tailored shade.
Apply trimming as desired.

'COOLIE' PLEATED SHADE

This shade is made like the pleated drum except that the top pleats are proportionately deeper and the bottom pleat barely tucked, or gently gathered, to accommodate the different circumferences of the two rings (Fig. 2).

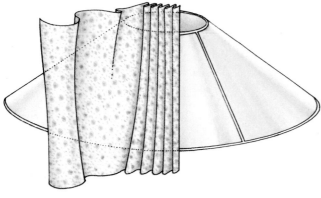

2. Pleat 'coolie' shape as for drum but space out bottom pleats.

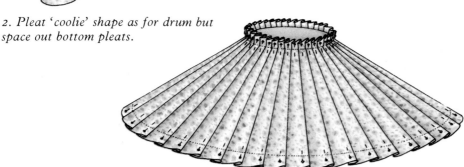

Right: draped or pleated fabric has a softened effect. Here it is pleated at the top and gently gathered at the bottom.

Paper shades

Lampshades in firm materials such as heavy paper and card are always popular and are especially well-suited to the contemporary domestic architecture and furnishing schemes of today. Paper in its various weights and qualities is inexpensive and such shades are quick and easy to make.

A fully-strutted frame is not necessary as the stiff paper or card produces the form quite simply when used with top and bottom rings only.

There are many interesting materials that can be used to make very handsome lampshades, notably parchment, buckram, decorated and plain card and some acetates.

Materials

You will need rings or strutted frames with correct fittings, binding tape, covering paper or card, scissors and craft knife, straight-edged metal ruler, 14–18 spring clothes pegs, glue (clear drying), needles and thread, trimmings and, for some paper shades, a hole punch and cord.

STRAIGHT-SIDED DRUM

Almost any stiff material can be used for a drum-shaped shade, particularly card or a buckram-backed fabric. This is a quick and easy form to make and lends itself to further decoration.

Being straight sided, two rings of exactly the same diameter must be used, one of which will support the required light fitting.

Estimating paper

Measure the outside circumference of one ring and decide the height of shade required. Add 13mm ($\frac{1}{2}$in) at one end for the side seam overlapped join.

Method

Bind each ring with tape. It is most important that the paper is very accurately cut, that edges are smooth and corners square. If preferred, make a pattern from thin card first to ensure the greatest accuracy.

Spread a very thin line of glue round the outside edge of one ring and peg the cover to it, but leave the seam overlap free.

Attach the other edge of the cover to the other ring similarly. The rings should be placed about 6mm ($\frac{1}{4}$in) in from the edge of the cover (Fig. 1).

Adjust side seam allowance, straighten and trim to overlap about 6mm ($\frac{1}{4}$in) and glue the join securely.

Now, using double white cotton thread, stitch upper and lower edges

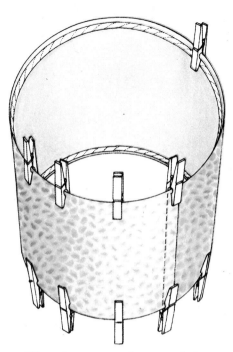

1. Glue, then peg card to taped ring.

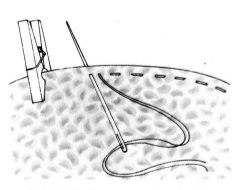

2. Stitch glued cover to tape on rings.

of cover to the tape on each ring (Fig. 2). Work small stitches on the inside where they will be visible and larger ones on the outside where they will be covered by the selected braid or trimming. Remove pegs as you go.

Trim is satisfactorily applied by glueing. (See page 63).

TAPERED PAPER SHADES

All tapered or conically shaped shades have a smaller ring at one end and a wider ring at the other end, in order to produce a sloping side. These shades may be made on a round, strutted frame or on two separate rings of different diameters. Using two rings allows a greater distance between the top and the bottom. In either case, it is essential to make a pattern first.

The covering must be firm paper, card or fabric covered buckram. It is made up in one piece with only one seam down the side.

Method

All rings and struts must be bound with tape.

There are two methods of making the pattern.

Method A. This is the simplest method to use for strutted, oval or round frames.

Place the bound frame on a large sheet of stiff paper with one strut lying flat on the paper. Make a mark on this first strut with chalk or a crayon for later identification.

Draw a line on the paper along one side of this marked strut from top to bottom.

Roll the frame slowly and carefully along the paper, marking each strut on the paper and also round the outer edges of the top and bottom rings (Fig. 1).

When the first strut is reached again, the pattern is complete.

Add 13mm (½in) down one side for seam overlap.

Re-roll the frame over the pattern and check for accuracy.

Cut out and peg pattern to the frame as for a drum shade, trim and adjust if necessary for a good fit.

Remove the pattern and cut out in the covering material.

Attach to the frame using the same method as for the drum shade described previously. Trim as desired.

Method B. This is for shades using rings only or a strutted frame having very tall sides.

Following Fig. 2, measure A to B, diameter of top ring. C to D, diameter of bottom ring, and E to F straight down through the centre of the 'bulb' ring (the height of the shade).

Make a diagram with all the measurements on a large sheet of paper (Fig. 3a).

Draw a line from D to B and extend it well up beyond B.

Draw another line from C to A and continue it on to cross the extended D-B line at G.

Make a large improvised 'compass' by cutting a strip of card (Fig. 3b) about 20mm (¾in) wide. Fix one end to G with a drawing pin.

Swing the card strip round to line up G, E and F, and punch out holes at E and F (see Fig. 3b).

With a pencil point through hole at F, and following Fig. 4, draw a wide arc. Draw another arc with pencil through top hole at E.

Measure the circumference of the bottom ring, then from C measure half that distance on the lower arc. Then measure the remaining half of the lower circumference to H.

Draw lines from G to C and G to H, crossing the upper arc at A and J. Add 13mm (½in) down one side (J to H) for seam over-lap. The pattern is now complete.

Cut out the pattern, peg to the frame or rings and adjust if necessary.

Mark and cut out in covering material and attach to the frame using the same method described for a drum shade.

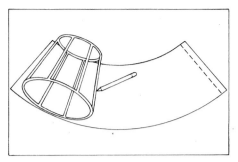

1. Making a shaped pattern, method A.

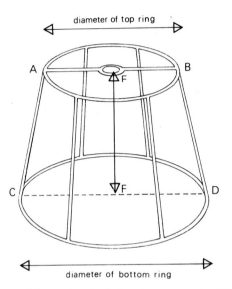

2. Measuring shade for pattern, method B.

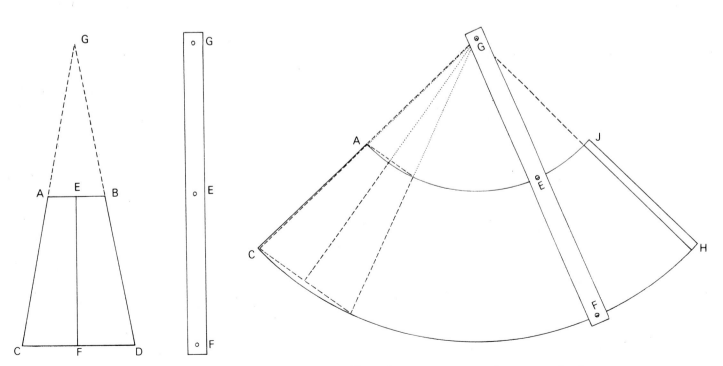

3a. Measurement diagram. 3b. 'Compass'. *4. Extend measurements as shown to make the pattern.*

59

This lampshade is very simple to make.
It is a circle of fabric with a hole cut
out in the centre the size of the top
ring, plus a seam allowance. The top is
hemmed and a frill attached while the
bottom is either hemmed, trimmed or
zigzag stitched. The lampshade frame
should have a fitted lining.

Pleated paper lampshades can be made
to cover a straight drum shape or a
tapered or conical shaped frame. The
method of construction is the same in
both cases. If the colours of paper
available are limited, or the shade must
match the colours in a room, then
wallpaper can be used, but size the
underside first.

PLEATED PAPER SHADES

Pleating paper demands the utmost accuracy and great patience. First attempts must be simple, but once the techniques are familiar, the scope is considerable.

Shades can be made on conical or cylindrical strutted frames, or on separate rings, but separate rings offer greater scope in size and shape.

Estimating paper

The correct amount of paper for pleating is important. If the length of the paper measures twice the circumference of the larger edge of the frame, then quite deep pleats can be made. The deeper the pleats, the more interesting and attractive are the shadow effects when lit up.

The width of the paper must be the height of the shade plus 50mm (2in) to allow the cover to extend 19mm (¾in) above the top of the frame and 31mm (1¼in) below the bottom ring.

Method

Bind the frame or rings to be used with tape.

Cut the covering material into a strip, measuring twice the circumference of the larger ring.

For 20mm (¾in) deep pleats, make folding marks at 20mm (¾in) intervals along top and bottom of paper and, using these marks as guides, fold the paper into concertina-like pleats (Fig. 1). The side of a ruler run down the folded edge will give a well-pronounced crease without damaging the paper.

Mark the centre of every pleat 20mm (¾in) from the top edge and 30mm (1¼in) from the bottom edge, then punch a hole through each mark (Fig. 2).

Overlap the ends of the pleated paper and glue them firmly together so that the seam is concealed neatly within a pleat. Allow the glue to dry thoroughly.

Cord. Thread a length of cord through the holes at the top, draw up to fit the top ring and stitch the ends together on the inside. Do not tie ends together as a knot will be ugly and bulky.

Attach the cord to the frame at the top first. Use white thread to match the tape. Take it round the ring and round the cord at the inside crease of the pleat (Fig. 3). Keeping the thread taut, work this lacing all round and fasten off firmly. At the same time care must be taken that the pleats are arranged evenly round the frame.

Attach the lower edge of the cover to the bottom ring in the same way.

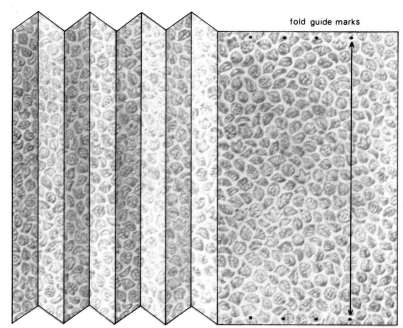

1. *Mark fold lines at regular intervals, then fold paper along the marks.*

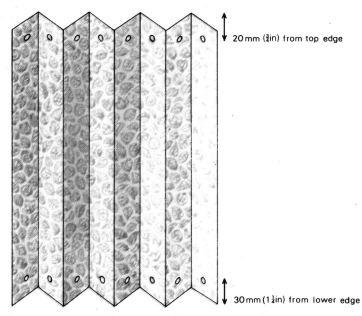

2. *Mark positions of holes centrally between folds, then punch out.*

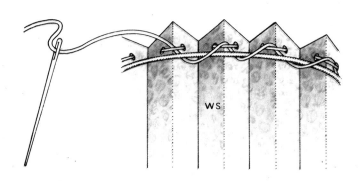

3. *Secure the shade to frame by stitching round cord and rings, as shown.*

62

TRIMMINGS

Trimming can enhance a shade or ruin it. Trimming is used to cover stitching and any raw edges of material but it must not detract from the lampshade. There is a multitude of commercially made braids, fringes, bindings and other suitable embellishments. These come in lovely colours, patterns and textures, and in various widths too. Trimming made of the same material or colour as the shade itself can be very satisfactory. This should be cut out on the bias, the edges folded inwards like bias binding. To avoid mistakes, a study of expensive shades in the lighting departments of stores might be time well-spent.

Trimmings are normally glued to paper, card and other rigid lampshades. Self-trimmed fabric edgings are often glued on as well, many fabric covers have trimming stitched on.

Sewing. All surplus material must be trimmed off the lampshade. Turn under 6mm ($\frac{1}{4}$in) of the end of braid and pin to edge of shade a little to one side of a strut. Stitch the braid as shown in Fig. 1, making a short stitch on the outside and a longer stitch at the back, between the braid and shade fabric. Continue sewing all round, turn last end under 6mm ($\frac{1}{4}$in) and

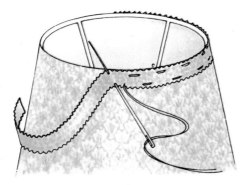

1. Stitching trimming to shade.

abut to starting end. Slip stitch ends together.

Do not stretch the trimming or sew it on too tightly or it will pull itself inside the ring and may even cause the covering fabric to pucker.

Glueing

Use a clear-drying glue and work only about 15cm (6in) at a time.

Apply a very thin layer of glue to the braid and press firmly to edge of shade until well adhered. Turn starting and finishing ends under 6mm ($\frac{1}{4}$in), glue down, then glue each to shade, abutting the folds closely together.

Press well to flatten, then leave for glue to set. A clothes peg is recommended to hold ends in place while drying out.

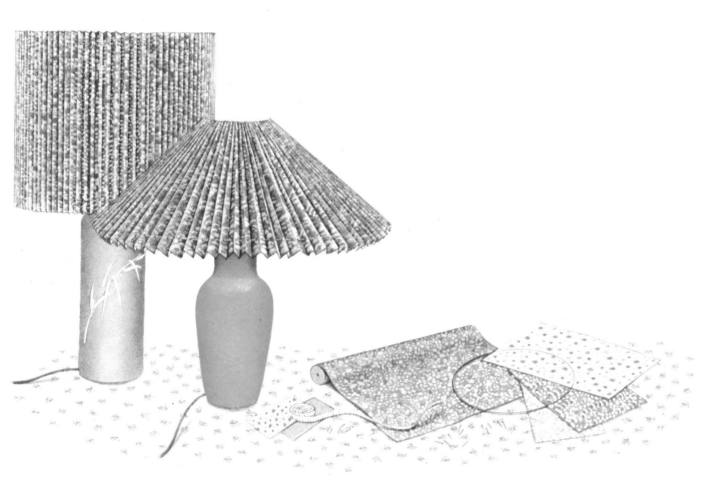

Blinds

Blinds, or shades, are one of the most practical forms of window treatment: light can be admitted or dispensed with literally by a flick of the wrist and – depending on whether there is a lining or backing – they can be opaque or translucent. As well as their useful applications, however, many blinds have distinctive decorative appeal and can hang in windows on their own, or combined with curtains.

There are three main types of blind which can be made from fabric. The roller blind (shade) is well-known but two lesser known variations are the Roman blind which is drawn up in pleats (shown opposite) and the Austrian blind which hangs in swags. Traditionally, Austrian blinds were made of sheer fabric and had ruffled scallops over the entire surface. But the type illustrated in this chapter is a modern variation. Gathered on a curtain heading, it hangs like a curtain when down and the swags are made by pulling the fabric up.

Before choosing a blind it is advisable to give some thought to which type will suit your needs. Easy-to-clean roller blinds are excellent devices for kitchens and bathrooms, while ruched Austrian blinds are suited to feminine bedrooms or sitting rooms, and Roman blinds complement modern, uncluttered surroundings.

The type of window is also important in the choice of blind. Roller blinds, for example, tend to suit utilitarian windows but their rather austere lines can often be effectively softened by combining them with curtains. The curtains do not have to be drawn (or made very full) since the blind fulfills the masking function. Roller blinds can also have shaped or trimmed edgings which increases their decorative potential.

Roman blinds, as a rule, are better in a dining room or sitting room than are roller blinds if they are used without curtains. Roman blinds have an elegant, tailored appearance, and can be used singly or, in instances where there are two or three windows together, side by side. Flat borders on the sides in a contrasting fabric can give additional importance to a Roman blind.

The Roman blind on the right, framed by curtains of the same fabric, makes the window a prominent decorative feature, yet integrates it with the colours and other fabrics in the room. As the blind is raised, the fabric forms pleats.

Ruched Austrian blinds are prettiest
when only partly drawn up. For this
reason, and because of their basically
feminine character, they combine well
66 with lace curtains.

Roller blinds

Various aids are available to make the task of roller blind-making easier. Roller blinds should be made of thin but fairly stiff, closely-woven fabric. Loosely-woven fabric tends to stretch and, if the fabric is too light, the edges of the blind will be wavy; if it is too heavy, it will make too thick a roll when the blind is up.

Special blind fabrics are available by the metre (yard) from many large department stores in a good range of colours, and are the quickest and easiest way to make a blind. These need no stiffening treatment. They usually have a spongeable, fade-resistant finish and do not fray.

Furnishing fabrics can usually be bought wide enough to make into roller blinds, but the fabric must be stiffened. If you do have to make joins, overlap the edges – matching any pattern – for about 1cm ($\frac{3}{8}$in) and glue together.

Fabric stiffeners make cloth stronger and can be bought in liquid form. Fabric is dipped into the liquid, or the liquid is painted on or sprayed on from an aerosol can. In the latter case, fabric must be well-sprayed on both sides.

Whichever type of stiffening is used, test a piece of fabric first to see how much is needed and how the fabric responds to it.

Iron-on or self-adhesive backing is best for strengthening small blinds but large blinds may become too heavy or too thick to roll, when backed. The backing should be placed on the fabric and pressed from the centre outwards to avoid crinkles.

PVC (plastic-coated) material is recommended for bathrooms and kitchens, as it can be sponged down.

Hardware. Rollers for blinds have two different ends; one end has a pin in it and the other has the winding mechanism (Fig. 1).

Most kits come with the pin cap unattached (Fig. 2), so it is easy to saw the roller to size, position the cap, and hammer home the pin. The roller may be marked with a guideline along its length where the fabric edge should be placed.

Two brackets (Fig. 3) come with the roller blind kit. One has a slot into which the winding mechanism fits, and the other has a round hole into which the pin end fits. These brackets have to be fixed to the side or face of the window frame, either inside the window recess or outside it, depending on the type of window.

Also in the kit is a wooden stretcher batten which fits through a hem at the foot of the blind to keep it straight, and a cord holder, plus 'acorn' or circular shaped handle for raising and lowering the blind.

For very long windows it is advisable to buy a heavy duty kit. In this the roller is larger in diameter than usual, with appropriate brackets, to take the extra bulk of fabric, and it has a stronger winding mechanism.

Measuring and estimating

Measure windows very carefully with a metal rule, not a cloth tape, as even a small inaccuracy can prevent a smooth fit.

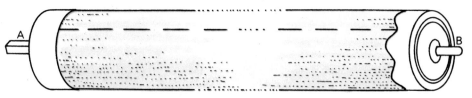

1. Rollers have a square pin on the left (A) (the winding mechanism) and a round pin on the right (B). Many have a line to show where to attach the blind.

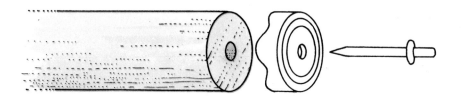

2. The round pin can be hammered home after the roller has been cut to size.

Measure from one recess of the window frame to the opposite recess. This will be the roller blind kit size, if the blind is to be recessed.

If fitting outside the recess, allow at least 2.5cm (1in) extra on either side of the window recess to prevent light streaks down the sides of the blind, and 5cm (2in) at the top of the recess so that the blind can roll freely.

If the right length roller is not obtainable, buy the next size up and cut it down to size. Many stores will do this for you.

The width of the fabric should equal the tip to tip length of the roller. Side turnings are not required because the edges of stiffened fabrics do not fray and, in any case, turnings would add too much bulk when the blind is rolled up. Measure the length of the window recess and add 30cm (12in), at least, to the length to allow for the roller to be covered when the blind is pulled down, and for the hem.

Method

Attaching the brackets. Mark the position of the brackets on the window frame and measure the distance between them. Bear in mind the difference between the bracket mounting and the bracket foot (Fig. 3). Screw in the brackets and saw the bare end of the roller to fit between the brackets, leaving sufficient length for the end cap and pin to fit into the bracket as well. Hammer home the pin.

Cutting. Before cutting the fabric, spread it out and have a good look at it. If it has a design on it, the pattern will have to be centred or the repeats

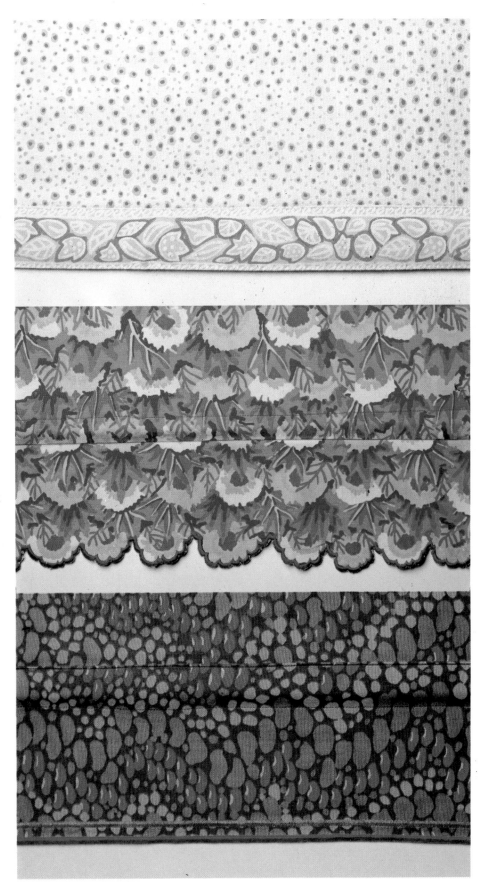

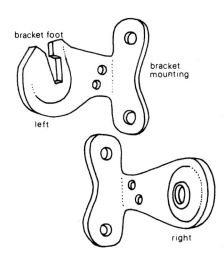

3. Always mount the bracket for the square pin on the left hand side of the window and the round pin on the right.

Three examples of roller blind edgings. Top: the batten is slotted through a border stitched on over the blind fabric. Middle: the blind has a zigzag stitched scallop border which follows the design of the pattern repeat. The batten is slotted between the main fabric and the lining (see overleaf). Bottom: in this version, zigzag stitching is applied in parallel lines. Stitching can also be continued along side edges to complete the border.

69

positioned so that they fall evenly over the blind.

Cut the fabric carefully, using a T-square to get accurate angles and a long batten or something similar for straight edges. Work with the fabric on a large flat table or the floor, to prevent creasing. Lay the fabric face down.

Batten. At this stage, a pocket should be made for the wooden batten which runs along the bottom to keep the blind firm and even. This can be stuck down or stitched.

To stick on the batten, spread adhesive on one side of the flat batten, place it on the wrong side of the fabric, then spread adhesive on the batten's other side (Fig. 4a), and on the fabric just below the batten.

Turn up the fabric and batten so that the batten cannot be seen, and weigh down lightly for awhile.

For a plain hem edge, turn 2.5cm (1in) to the wrong side of the blind and stitch, then slide the batten into this pocket (Fig. 4b).

For blinds that are to have a decorative edging, the pocket for the batten can be a tuck sewn higher on the shade, leaving the bottom free for decoration (Fig. 4c). Batten pockets can be strengthened with iron-on backing.

Attaching blind to the roller

If the roller does not have a guideline draw one with a pencil.

Stick the top of the blind along this guideline with adhesive tape, check for straightness and nail the blind to the roller with very small tacks (Fig. 5). When the blind is finished, screw a cord holder to the centre of the batten (Fig. 6).

Adjusting tension

When the roller has been slotted into the brackets (square pin into the slotted bracket and the round pin into the round-holed bracket) it may be necessary to adjust the tension.

To make sure the blind has accurate tension, place it in the brackets, then pull it down as far as it will go.

Carefully remove blind and roller from the brackets, taking care not to release the ratchet. With the blind out of its brackets, re-wind it by hand and replace it.

Pull the blind down once again. If you feel that it now has enough tension and returns to its fully rolled position easily, leave it. But if tighter tension is needed, repeat as above until it works satisfactorily.

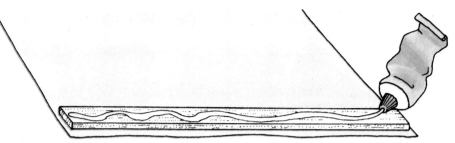

4a. Glue batten to wrong side of fabric. Spread glue on back of batten and on fabric below batten. Roll up to enclose batten.

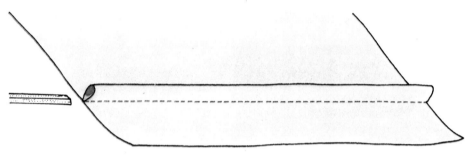

4b. For a stitched batten casing, turn hem in to wrong side and stitch down. Insert batten.

4c. For a decorative roller blind edging, sew a tuck higher up and wide enough to take batten.

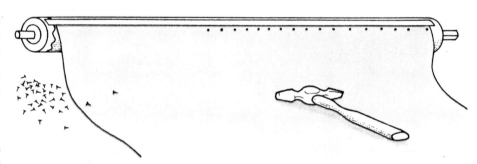

5. Stick blind to roller with adhesive tape, then secure with small tacks.

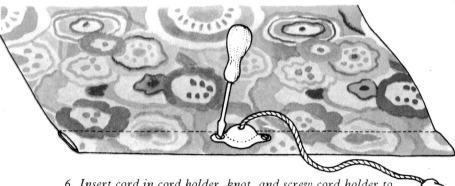

6. Insert cord in cord holder, knot, and screw cord holder to batten on right or wrong side.

DECORATIVE EDGINGS

Bottom edges of roller blinds can be decorated with many different types of trimming, such as a fringe, bobble braid or rows of ribbon. Stick or sew these trimmings on, depending on the fabric of the blind.

Some fabric designs lend themselves to a cut-out design, with a brass rod pushed through the bottom instead of a wooden batten. You can also shape the bottom edge of a blind beneath the batten by cutting out half circles, squares or what you will.

Hand-painted designs look pleasing on a plain blind. Use fabric paints for this. Tie-and-dye or batik are two other techniques.

Shaped edging

In addition to the measured blind fabric, you will need a strip of paper and additional blind fabric of the following dimensions: blind width $\times$ batten depth + 3cm (1in) + depth of blind (edging) below batten. If using furnishing fabric, you will also need iron-on interfacing the same size as the paper. (8cm (3in) is an average depth for edging below the batten.)

To make a paper pattern for the shaped edging, draw lines on the paper to indicate the depth of the batten, starting 2.5cm (1in) from the top; draw the shape on the remaining section (Fig. 7), and cut out.

Stiffened fabrics. Cut a strip of blind fabric to the same *overall* size as the paper pattern.

Draw the batten allowance on the strip's wrong side.

Apply adhesive *below* this area and stick the strip to the back of the blind. Then apply paper pattern, mark outline and cut out edging (Fig. 8a).

Apply adhesive to both sides of the batten, insert between the free part of the strip and the blind, and stick down (Fig. 8b). Stick the remaining free edge of the strip to the blind.

Unstiffened fabrics. Apply interfacing to the wrong side of the cut out strip (see above). Pin the strip on the blind with right sides together and place the pattern on top (Fig. 9).

Draw the shaped pattern with tailor's chalk, remove pattern and machine stitch 5mm ($\frac{1}{4}$in) inside the line. Cut along the line, snip into the turnings (Fig. 10) and turn right side out.

Turn under the free edge of the strip 5mm ($\frac{1}{4}$in) and machine stitch to blind.

Work a second line of stitching below, leaving the batten width plus 5mm ($\frac{1}{4}$in) for the batten casing (Fig. 11).

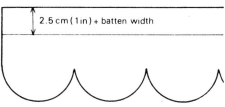

7. *Draw line to mark batten width, plus 2.5cm (1in). Draw edging pattern below.*

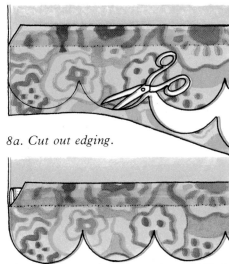

8a. *Cut out edging.*

8b. *Glue batten between strip and blind.*

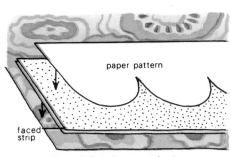

9. *Unstiffened fabrics: apply interfacing to fabric strip, pin with pattern to blind.*

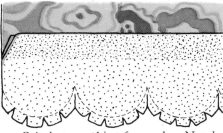

10. *Stitch 5mm ($\frac{1}{4}$in) from edge. Notch.*

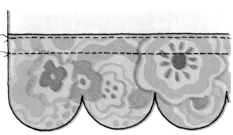

11. *Turn edging inside out, press. Turn under free edge. Sew batten casing.*

Cut out edging

Make a paper pattern and allow extra fabric and interfacing for this as for the edging already described, but mark the allowance for the batten casing from the *bottom* edge of the strip (Fig. 12).

Stiffened fabrics. Apply the strip and cut out the shapes as for the shaped edging, but stick the strip completely to the back of the blind.

Turn up the batten casing allowance without creasing, apply adhesive to the right side of the segments along the edges and stick to the back of the blind (Fig. 13a). Insert the batten rod.

Unstiffened fabrics. Apply interfacing to the strip and stitch as for shaped edging.

Turn up the batten allowance, fold under the raw edge for 3mm ($\frac{1}{8}$in) and machine stitch to the blind (Fig. 13b). Insert the batten rod (Fig. 14).

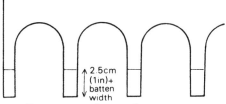

12. *For cut out edge, make paper pattern with batten casing at lower edge.*

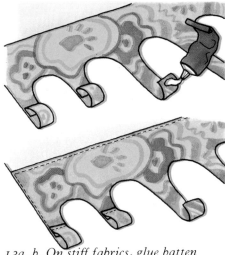

13a, b. *On stiff fabrics, glue batten casing; stitch unstiffened fabrics.*

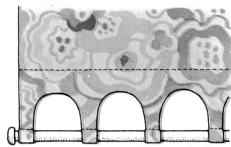

14. *Insert the batten rod in the glued or stitched slots to complete blind.* 71

Roman blinds

These pull to the top of the window like roller blinds but they need more space at the top since they pleat rather than roll. Therefore the fabric does not have to be as stiff as that used for roller blinds, though it does need to be firmly woven.

Rings are attached to the back of the blind, through which cords are threaded to pull the blind up (Fig. 1); and the blind is attached to a wooden heading board.

Roman blinds should be lined.

Measuring and estimating

Measure the width and length of the window, allowing 3cm (1in) extra for side turnings and 15cm (6in) extra for top and bottom turnings.

Materials

You will need fabric and lining, small brass or plastic rings - enough to make rows 30cm (12in) apart horizontally and 15cm (6in) apart vertically over the area of the blind, and enough binding tape to make the vertical rows. Non-stretch cord for each vertical row of rings plus threading down the side

as illustrated; a screw eye for each row of cords, plus one slightly larger screw eye to take all ends, are required. You will also need a piece of wood, measuring 2.5cm × 5cm (1in × 2in) and cut to the width of the blind, for a heading board; a metal rod or batten the width of the blind and a cleat to tie the blind cords to, when it is in place; angle irons and screws for mounting the heading board.

Method

Cut fabric and lining the same size.

With right sides together, pin, tack (baste) and sew the lining to the main fabric down the sides and along the bottom, taking 15mm (½in) seams (Fig. 2). Turn to the right side and press.

On the reverse side of the blind, mark parallel lines for batten casing. Begin 14cm (5½in) from the bottom edge (see Fig. 1). Baste (tack) along lines (Fig. 3).

Following Fig. 1, mark lines for the tape, keeping them even and parallel. The first line should be 15mm (½in) from the sides. The subsequent rows should be equidistant, roughly 30cm

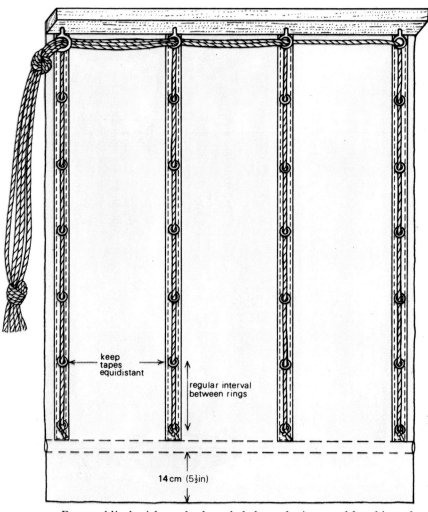

keep
tapes
equidistant

regular interval
between rings

14 cm (5½in)

1. Roman blind with cords threaded through rings and head board.

(12in) apart. Tape lines start at top of batten casing, as shown.

Position tape along lines and stitch it down along both its edges. Sew through fabric *and* lining. Turn under raw ends at top and bottom and stitch down. Sew rings on the tape by hand (Fig. 4) and at regular intervals. The first rings should be 15mm (½in) from the top of the batten case. Other rings should be spaced evenly along each line of tape. All rings must be parallel.

Machine stitch batten casing lines then unpick one end, A–B in Fig. 5.

Slot the batten rod in the casing and slip-stitch the ends together (Fig. 5).

Fixing board. Screw in the eyes on the underside of the wooden heading board, (see Fig. 6), one positioned above each vertical row of rings, with a larger screw eye on the right-hand side of the board to help bear the weight of the pulling cords.

Attach the top of the blind to the top of the wooden heading, with tacks or staples (Fig. 7).

Attaching cords. Cut lengths of cord twice the length of the blind, plus its length to the right-hand edge.

With the blind laid flat on a table, tie the cords to the appropriate bottom rings (Fig. 8) and thread vertically through the rings and up through the screw eyes as shown in Fig. 9. Knot the cords together about 2.5cm (1in) from the outside edge of the blind, near the top outside screw eye. Mount the wooden heading board at the top of the window in angle irons (Fig. 10).

Cut the cords so that they are all level at the bottom edge and knot them again. Fix the cleat to the window to hold the cords when the blind is up.

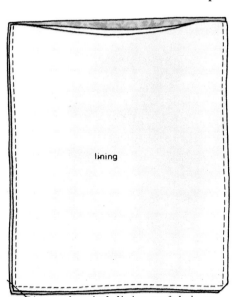

2. Pin, tack, stitch lining to fabric on sides and bottom. Clip corners.

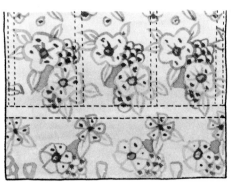

3. Stitch batten casing and vertical tapes. Sew through all layers.

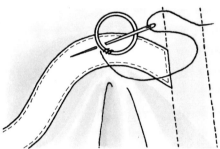

4. Stitch rings on vertical tapes, spacing them evenly.

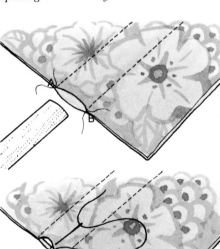

5. Unpick from A to B at one end of batten casing. Insert batten and slip stitch the end together again.

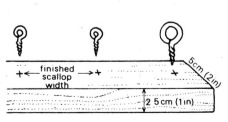

6. Screw in eyes on underside of heading board at positions parallel to tapes. Screw large eye in on right.

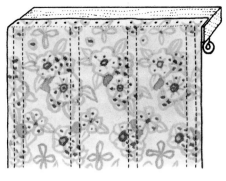

7. Attach blind to heading board with tacks or staples.

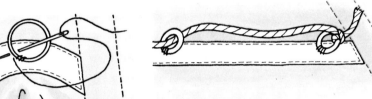

8. With blind flat on table tie cords to bottom rings and thread vertically.

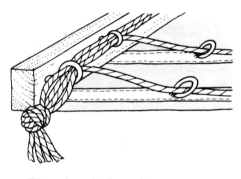

9. Thread cords through screw eyes, to the right. Knot cords together outside the blind edge.

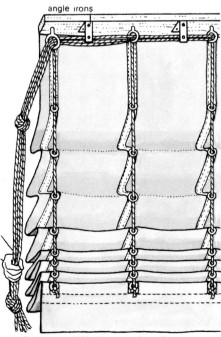

10. Draw up blind to make pleats. 73

Austrian blinds

These soft ruched blinds work on much the same principle as Roman blinds, in that they are drawn up on cords threaded through rings and suspended from a wooden heading board, but they are made of light fabrics, are usually unlined and have gathered or pleated curtain headings as well as scalloped swags.

Measuring and estimating

The amount of fabric needed depends on how many scallops are to be in the blind, how shirred an effect is required and also on the weight of the fabric being used. Scallops should, as a rule, not be more than 30cm (12in) wide. As a rough guide, measure the width of the window and add 3cm (1in) extra for side hems. Then double measurement of width of window (or multiply $2\frac{1}{2}$ times for a very full swag).

If the fabric has to be seamed to make the right width, allow an extra 2.5cm (1in) for french seams.

To estimate the length, measure the length of the window and add another 20cm (8in).

Materials

Small plastic or brass curtain rings are needed and enough hem binding tape for each vertical row of rings.

Non-stretch cord and a screw eye are also required for each vertical row of rings, and choice of curtain heading tape and curtain hardware. Gathered or pencil pleats are recommended. (See curtain chapter for details.)

A piece of wood, measuring 2.5cm × 5cm (1in × 2in), cut to the width of the blind and two angle irons are needed for a heading board; also a cleat to tie the blind cords to, when it is in place.

Method

Cut out the fabric and hem sides and bottom. Slipstitch top.

A frill can also be added (see Sewing Guide for instructions).

Lay the blind flat on the floor, wrong side up, and mark positions of tape over the side hems and vertically down the body of the blind at regular intervals – depending on the number of scallops planned. Remember that the distance between the tapes will be at least double that of the intended swag or scallop.

Stitch the tape in place along both its edges (Fig. 1).

Sew the curtain rings at even intervals down the tape, the first about 15cm (6in) down from the top of the blind, the others about 20cm (8in) apart. The last should be about 6cm ($2\frac{1}{2}$in) up from the hemmed bottom edge (see Fig. 1). Make sure the rings are aligned evenly horizontally.

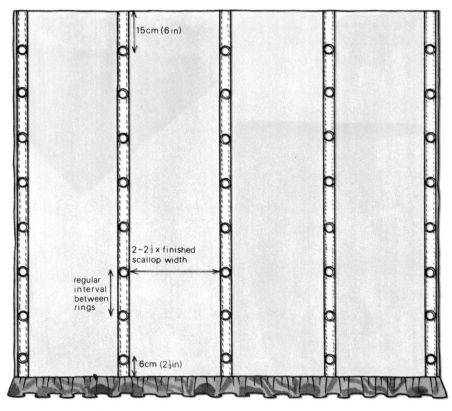

15cm (6in)

2–2½ × finished scallop width

regular interval between rings

6cm (2½in)

1. *Mark positions of tapes and rings, stitch down tapes, then rings, at regular intervals.*

74

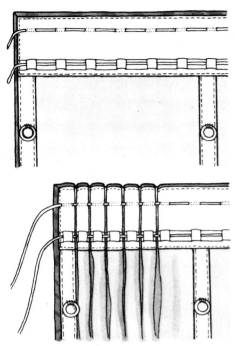

2a and b. Sew curtain heading tape to wrong side of blind. Gather heading.

Headings. The blind will now be too wide for the window.

Sew curtain heading tape to the wrong side of the blind (Fig. 2) and pleat or gather it on the tape until it is the width of the window (see Curtain Chapter for detailed instructions.)

String the blind with cords as for the Roman blind, tying each cord to the first ring at the bottom of each tape.

Mounting. Mount curtain track on the *front* of the heading board, as in Fig. 3, and attach screw eyes along the under side of the board at positions parallel to the rows of tape.

Run cords through screw eyes, as described for Roman blinds, then mount the blind on the curtain track and fix the heading board in the window with angle irons.

Pull cords and swags will form.

3. Mount curtain track on front of board, attach screws underneath.

Austrian blinds, like curtains, are at least twice as wide as the windows they decorate and, like curtains, the extra width is accommodated by gathered or pleated headings. This produces a lush and fulsome swag when the blind is raised. The example shown here has a pencil pleated heading and a frill, made in the same fabric. The effect is decidedly one of ruffled charm.

Curtains

Curtains serve three main purposes: they provide a screen for privacy, a form of insulation and they are an important part of home design.

The amount of screening may be minimal; for example, sheer net curtains which prevent passers-by seeing in; or it may be greater, such as heavy velvet or brocade curtains drawn across the window at night. Shower curtains provide privacy too, but their main purpose is to prevent water splashing. For extra warmth or insulation (and a tidy appearance from outside) curtains may be lined with a plain fabric or even interlined with a layer of thick, soft fabric between the curtain and lining. Bed curtains, though mainly decorative in modern homes, can also be used for their original insulating purpose.

Numerous design effects can be created by curtains. They can be used to soften angles and to change the apparent size of windows and even of the room itself. Choice of fabric can affect the importance of windows in a room by causing them to predominate or blend with the surroundings.

Headings. These refer to the different gathering or pleating styles at the top of curtains. In this chapter headings are described separately and unlined curtains (described page 84) serve as the basic curtain method. Lined curtains are a variation of them.

FABRICS

Traditional curtain fabrics include velvet, brocade, linen and cotton/linen mixtures as well as crisp cottons (plain, printed or gingham). Besides these fabrics, there is a wide range of synthetic materials, some loosely woven, some heavier, including fibreglass. The choice depends on the style of the room in which the curtains are to hang.

Lining. To extend the life of the curtains, to prevent unnecessary light coming through and to give a neat appearance to the curtains from the outside, lining is recommended.

Furnishing lining is available in a number of colours and it is even possible to buy a metallic, woven lining for extra insulation.

Interlining gives extra body and insulation to curtains, as well as a very luxurious finish. The fabric used for interlining is soft and loosely woven – bump or domette are the usual choices, although flannelette is sometimes used.

Café curtains are one of the simplest curtain styles. Here a decorative pleated frill adds special character.

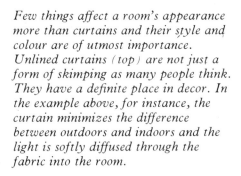

Few things affect a room's appearance more than curtains and their style and colour are of utmost importance. Unlined curtains (top) are not just a form of skimping as many people think. They have a definite place in decor. In the example above, for instance, the curtain minimizes the difference between outdoors and indoors and the light is softly diffused through the fabric into the room.

The gathered valance (above) reduces the void which such a large window could create.

The bed curtains with pinch-pleated headings are self-lined. Bow tie-backs emphasize the feminine appearance.

The richness of the bedroom curtains (right) is caused by both fullness and interlining. The broadness of the window is reduced by joining the curtains at the top.

The elegant pinch-pleated curtains
above have tapered tie-backs
(described page 95). Since tie-backs
usually stay in position, sheer curtains
have been added to screen the interior
and to mask the visual break caused by
the window sill. Note the different
effects achieved by the two headings
above and left.

Treating a door and a window together.

Café curtains are used here to give the window depth.

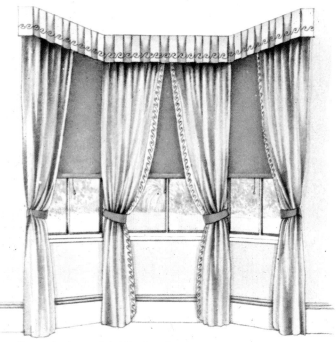

Bay window with blinds (shades) and curtains.

Generous curtain widths broaden the appearance of a narrow window.

Curtains can be kept away from an arched window, or a valance used to emphasize it.

A curtain for a summer day.

The main criteria when selecting a style of curtain are the shape of the window and the room it is in. For example, it is possible to use your curtains to alter the appearance of a room's proportions. The window can be made to look bigger by hanging floor-to-ceiling curtains or a more cottage-style look can be achieved by café curtains or by hanging sill-length curtains. The sketches opposite give some idea of how different treatments suit different windows but one point to bear in mind is that windows are there to provide light, and curtains should not be hung so that they screen the window during the day.

The diagram below shows the choice of hanging positions.

Headings

As well as length, breadth and hanging position, the choice of heading is crucially important. Headings vary from a simple casing through which to slot a rod or expanding wire, to intricately sewn pleats. One of the most popular types of heading involves the use of curtain tapes which gather or facilitate pinch pleating, but hand-sewn headings are highly regarded.

Borders and trimmings

A plain curtain may be trimmed with braid or flat trimming which is usually positioned round the inner and lower edges. (It is not usually applied across the top of the curtain as the crispness would be lost in the pleats or gathers across the top.)

Trimming may also be used to emphasize the height of the window, by applying it down the sides only.

Trimming, applied down the inner edges of the curtains, can be particularly effective if the curtains are held to the side with tie-backs.

Pelmets and valances

Pelmets and valances fit over curtain headings and serve to hide tracks, to lend height or a specially decorative appearance to the window. Both are described in detail further on.

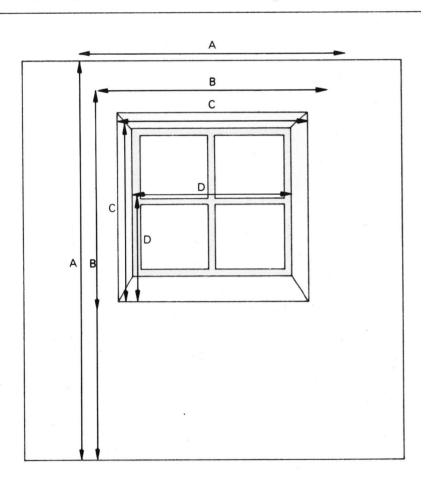

AA: Measurements for floor to ceiling curtains
BB: Measurements for wall fixed curtains, either sill or floor length
CC: Measurements for curtains inside the window recess
DD: Measurements for café curtains

Accessories

The choice of tracks, rods, tapes, hooks and so on is an important factor in determining the final look of curtains. The choice ranges from wooden poles, with wooden rings, to plain white tracks with invisible runners slotted behind the track.

Consider the weight of the fabric to be used before deciding on the hardware, as some of the simpler track mechanisms are not suitable for heavy-weight fabrics.

Tracks

Before buying a track, decide whether it is to be fitted to the wall, to the ceiling or the roof of the window reveal. If a wall-fitting type is chosen, it must be decided whether the track should show or not when the curtains are closed. If there is to be a pelmet or valance round the top of the curtain, the track need not be elaborate. Several styles of tracks are shown here in combination with various runners and hooks.

On bay or bow windows, the track must bend sufficiently to fit round the curves of the window.

Runners. Once the track or rod has been chosen, the selection of runners is limited. There is usually a particular shape to go with a particular track. These runners include traditional rings in wood, plastic or brass to hang on rods or poles; runners in plastic or brass which hang from the widest section of a specially shaped track; plain or decorative runners which hang from a smooth track; and small runners which slot into the back of a specially shaped, plain-looking track (Fig. 1).

Some runners glide along a plain plastic track, with the hook attached to the runner in such a way that when the curtain is hung, the top of the curtain covers the track and the runners. One type of runner combines an extra loop to hold the hooks on the lining at the same time (Fig. 2).

When a valance is also hung, the track is a little more intricate (Fig. 3).

Another variation is the track which is in the form of a decorative pole, with runners which are attached to curtain rings (Fig. 4). The rings may be traditional wooden rings, but many modern tracks are made to fit flush against a wall with imitation rings attached to the runners.

As a general rule, allow one hook and runner per 10cm (4in) curtain width, plus one extra for the edge.

The runner at the outer end of the curtain is constructed in a different way, so that it can be anchored to the track - it is an end stop rather than a runner.

One feature that runners have in common is that they have loops through which to slot the hooks which will be attached to the curtains.

Hooks

Hooks are attached to the curtain heading at one end and through the runners on the rod or track, at the other end. The most common type of hook, for use with draw-string tapes, is made of plastic or metal and has a double bend, plus a small extra bend to hold it in place. (Fig. 5a).

An alternative type of hook is one with prongs, which is slotted into a specially designed tape to make pinch pleats (Fig. 5b). The prongs are quite long and have the advantage of stiffening the heading as well as forming a pleat.

For hand-gathered headings it is possible to buy brass hooks (5c and d), or pronged hooks of various lengths, which do not need stitching.

Tapes

Most headings have some form of curtain tape, and those which gather or enable pencil or pinch pleats to be made without stitching (Figs. 6–8) are very popular.

Before buying fabric, decide on the type of heading tape you wish to use as this determines the width of fabric needed for the curtains.

The height of the curtain above the track may be adjusted by using tapes so that the slots for the hooks are at the top or the bottom of the tape - which may be up to about 8cm (3½in) deep. Some tapes have several rows of slots so that the positions of the hooks may be altered once the curtains are put up (see Fig. 7).

In some cases, it is a good idea to position the tape a few centimetres (a couple of inches) from the top of the curtain and to stiffen the part of the curtain above the tape to give the curtain extra height.

Weights

There are various types of weights on the market to help fabrics hang well. The main choice (*right*) is between a string of weights - either a chain or a series of them in a strip of fabric casing - which is slotted into the hem when it is taken up, and circular weights (coins make a suitable substitute) which are sewn into the corners of the curtain as the hems are mitred.

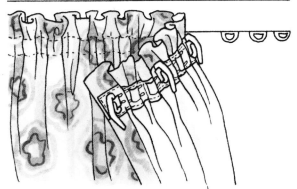

1. A standard tape for a gathered heading attached to runners below a plain plastic track.

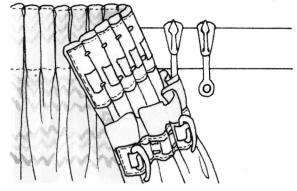

2. Runners designed to take a detachable lining, with the pencil-pleated heading covering the runners.

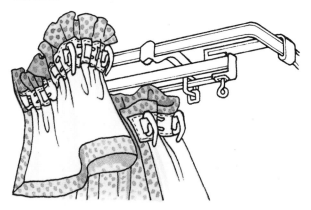

3. No runners are needed for this pelmet track – the hooks loop over the narrow rail.

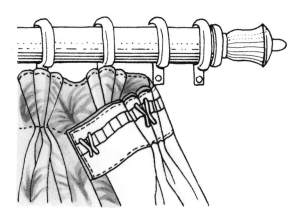

4. Pinch pleats look particularly effective hung from a decorative pole.

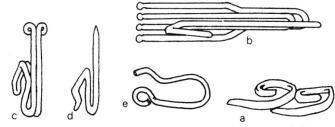

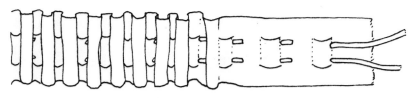

5. Hooks for hand-pleated, slotted tape and gathered headings.

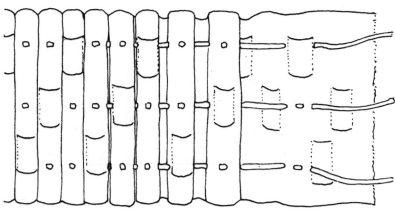

6. A standard tape for a simple gathered heading.

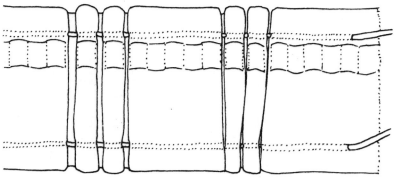

7. Pencil pleated tape with three rows of slots for attaching hooks.

8. Tape for a drawstring, pinch-pleated heading.

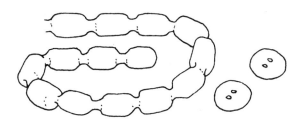

Weights may be slotted into a tape which runs through the hem, or single weights used at corners.

Unlined curtains

All styles and types of curtains described in this chapter are derivations of the basic unlined curtain described here. Therefore, before attempting to undertake any curtain project it is necessary to become familiar with the construction of unlined curtains.

Measuring and estimating fabric

The first two points to sort out when making curtains are the type of heading and the overall size. These two together dictate the amount of fabric you will need.

When measuring the window, it is essential to put up the track or rod first, so that the exact height and width can be taken. If possible, extend the track beyond the window itself so that when the curtains are drawn back during the day they will not exclude light.

Once you have decided how to hang the curtains in relation to the track, you can take the final measurements – measuring the actual area the curtains are to cover.

Multiply the width of the area by the appropriate figure for the heading you have chosen ($1\frac{1}{2}$ for a simple gathered heading, $2\frac{1}{2}$ for a pencil-pleated heading and so on – see headings, pages 88–94). Divide this figure into two if the window is to have a pair of curtains rather than a single panel and add 10–15cm (4–6in) to each curtain width if the curtains are to overlap at the centre. If there is a return on the outer edge, add its depth. This gives the width of one *finished flat* curtain. Add 6cm ($2\frac{1}{2}$in) at each side for hems.

Fabric widths. Work out how many widths of fabric are needed by dividing the width of the curtain by the width of the fabric chosen, allowing an extra 1.5cm ($\frac{1}{2}$in) seam allowance on each side of each fabric width after the first. Use complete widths of fabric for the panels which will be at the centre of the window and the cut sections for the side panels.

For the length of the curtain, measure the actual length the curtain is to cover. Add an extra 15cm (6in) for the hem and 7.5cm (3in) for the heading (see diagram below).

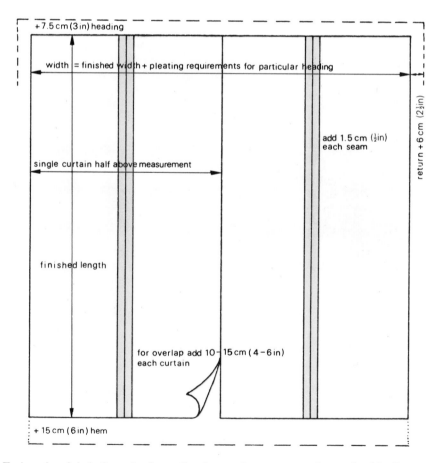

Estimating fabric for a basic, unlined curtain : measure size and add allowances indicated for seams, hems, overlap, return and pleating or gathering.

Patterned fabric. If you have chosen a patterned fabric, allow extra for matching the pattern, depending on the depth of the pattern repeat and the number of widths of fabric you need for the pair of curtains (see Sewing Guide).

To calculate how much extra fabric you will need, each length must have a complete number of pattern repeats. If the curtains are 155cm (62in) long, and the pattern repeat is 50cm (20in) you will need to allow 200cm (80in) for each length of fabric, so a pair of curtains made from three widths of fabric (as in Fig. 1) will need 6m (240in or 6⅝yd). Fig. 2 shows how to match the pattern when joining fabric widths and sections. Lay one piece of fabric flat, right side up. Turn under the selvedge on the piece to be joined and press. Lay the second piece right side up next to the first. Match the pattern and pin along the crease line.

With floor to ceiling curtains, arrange the pattern repeat so that it starts at the top of the curtain. With sill-length curtains, the lower edge is more visible, so arrange the pattern so that the repeat ends at hem level (Fig. 3).

Method

Cutting out. It is vitally important that curtains be cut straight across the fabric and any mistake may cause them to hang unevenly.

On straight-woven fabrics, it is advisable to withdraw a thread or two across the width of the cloth and use this as a cutting line.

Linen, chintz and most cotton prints have a movable grain and the fabric stretches slightly as it is printed so that the pattern is not straight either. In these cases, use a set square and cut at right angles to the selvedges.

Making up. Start by joining the necessary number of fabric widths. Use a flat seam with 1.5cm (½in) seam allowances. Clip into the seam allowance (particularly if it is a selvedge) every 10-15cm (4-6in) down the length of the seam. Press the seam open (Fig. 4).

Turn in 3cm (1¼in) deep double hems down each side and slipstitch (see Sewing Guide) in place.

Turn up and slipstitch a double hem 12.5cm (3in) deep along the bottom (Fig. 5), mitring corners (see Sewing Guide) and enclosing weights if necessary (Fig. 6).

Turn top of curtain fabric down 7.5cm (3in) to wrong side.

Finally, apply the heading chosen, following instructions in this chapter.

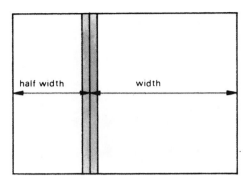

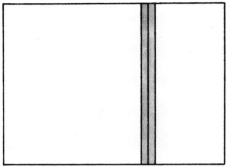

1. When joining widths, position complete widths at the centre.

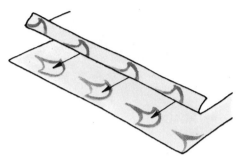

2. Make sure that the pattern matches at the seam lines.

3. Choose where to start the pattern repeats before cutting out.

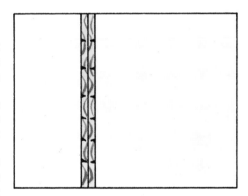

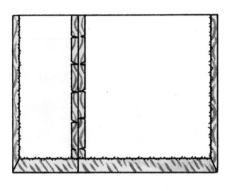

4. Clip allowances to prevent puckers.

5. Slipstitch hems in place.

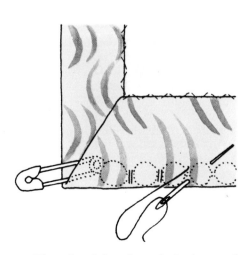

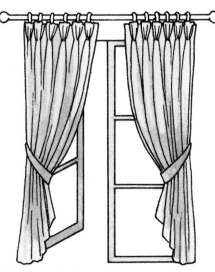

6. Thread weights through the hem and stitch in place to anchor them.

Simple unlined curtains.

Lined curtains

There is a choice of methods when it comes to making lined curtains. A loose or 'bagged' lining is the most common form but a preferable method - and necessary for velvet or wide curtains - is a 'locked in' lining. The third style involves a washable, detachable lining.

Handsewn headings. If you intend to make a handsewn heading for any of the lined curtains described below, remember to interface the curtain as described on page 90.

LOOSE LININGS
Estimating fabric
The curtain fabric should be 12cm (5in) wider and 22.5cm (9in) longer than the finished flat curtain. The lining should be the same size as the finished flat curtain.

Making up
Join fabric widths as described for unlined curtains.

Position the lining on the curtain fabric with right sides together and side edges matching. The top of the lining should be 7.5cm (3in) below the top of the curtain fabric.

Stitch side seams, taking 1.5cm (½in) seam allowances, but leave 20cm (7in) unstitched at the lower edge (Fig. 1). Surplus curtain fabric will form a small pleat at this stage. Clip the seam turnings.

Turn up and stitch double 7.5cm (3in) hem on main fabric (Fig. 2). Machine stitch double hem on lining totalling 5cm (2in).

Turn curtain right side out, matching centres so a margin of curtain fabric shows on each side of lining - slip-stitch the remaining part of the lining to the curtain at the edges (Fig. 3).

Turn the top of the curtain over the lining fabric and mitre the corners (Fig. 4). Turn in the raw edge if necessary, or position curtain tape over the raw edge of the curtain fabric.

LOCKED-IN LINING
Estimating fabric
The curtain fabric should be 12cm (5in) wider than the ungathered curtain and 22.5cm (9in) longer. The lining should be 4cm (1½in) smaller on all sides than the finished flat curtain.

Making up
Join all seams as described for unlined curtains.

Turn in 6cm (2½in) down the sides of the curtain fabric and 15cm (6in) across lower edge, mitring corners. Use a large hemstitch (Fig. 1).

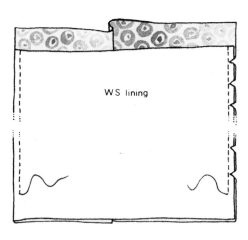

1. Stitch the side seams, joining the lining to the curtain.

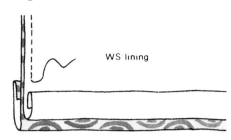

2. Turn up hems on curtain and lining, ensuring lining is shorter than curtain.

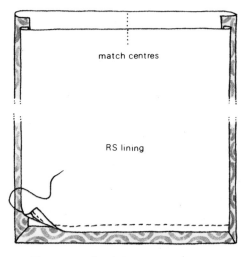

3. Turn curtain right side out, matching centre of lining to centre of curtain.

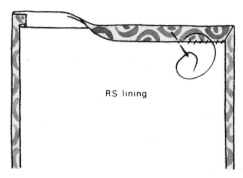

4. Turn top of curtain over lining. For curtains with a tape heading, the raw edge can be tacked (basted) in place. Hem hand-pleated curtains.

1. Turn in sides and hem of curtain and stitch with large hemstitch.

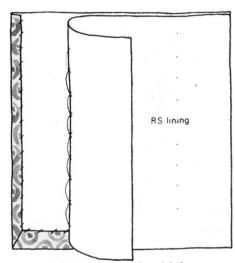

RS lining

2. Lock lining to curtain with loose stitches.

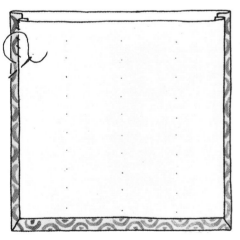

3. Slipstitch the lining to the curtain down the sides, for a neat finish.

Using tailor's chalk, make vertical lines down wrong side of curtain fabric 30cm (12in) apart.

Place the lining fabric over the curtain, with wrong sides together, positioning the top of the lining 2cm ($\frac{3}{4}$in) from the top of the curtain.

Fold back the lining 30cm (12in) from the right hand edge. Lock the lining into the curtain, picking up only a single thread from each layer of fabric (Fig. 2). The stitches should be about 10cm (4in) apart and should start 15cm (6in) from the top of the curtain. Do not pull the thread tight between stitches as this may pucker the fabric. Work further lines of stitching 30cm (12in) apart.

On the lining press 2cm ($\frac{3}{4}$in) turnings down sides and 4cm ($1\frac{1}{2}$in) at lower edge. Slipstitch lining to hem allowance of curtain (Fig. 3).

Turn in 7.5cm (3in) at top of curtain and 6.5cm ($2\frac{1}{2}$in) at top of lining, mitring corners.

Slipstitch lining to curtain across the top of the curtain and apply the heading.

INTERLINING

This gives curtains extra body and insulation. Even if you do not interline the whole curtain, it is worth putting a facing of interlining behind the heading for extra body, particularly if the heading is gathered by hand.

Estimating fabric

The amounts of curtain fabric and lining fabric are the same as described for curtains with a locked-in lining. The amount of interlining needed (bump or domette) is exactly the same as the finished flat curtain.

Making up

Join widths of fabric for the curtain and lining as described for unlined curtains.

Join the interlining pieces by overlapping the raw edges by 1.5cm ($\frac{1}{2}$in), with the wrong side of one section over the right side of the other section. Join with two rows of backstitch (Fig. 4).

Lock the interlining into the curtain as described for lining, positioning the interlining as in Fig. 5.

Turn the edges of the curtain fabric over the interlining down the sides and across the lower edge and catchstitch (see Sewing Guide) in place, mitring the corners.

Apply the lining to the interlined curtain and turn in as described for locked-in lining.

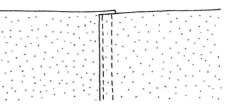

4. Overlap interlining to join it.

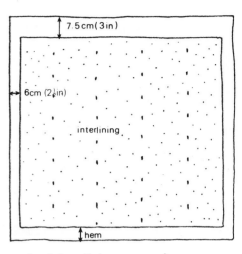

5. Lock interlining to curtain.

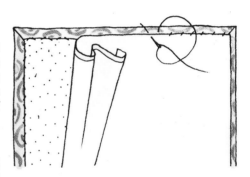

6. Turn in top of the lining.

Fold down the top of the curtain over the interlining, turning in the corners slightly. Turn in the top of the lining 6.5cm ($2\frac{1}{2}$in) and slipstitch in place (Fig. 6). Apply the chosen heading.

DETACHABLE LINING

The simplest way of attaching a detachable lining is to use a curtain tape at the top of the lining as well as the top of the curtain.

Estimating fabric

Estimate the fabric for both the lining and the curtain as described for lined curtains.

Making up

Make up the curtains and linings separately as described for unlined curtains, attaching a draw-string type tape to the curtain itself and a special lining tape to the top of the lining.

Headings

CURTAINS WITH CASED HEADINGS

Some net curtains, café curtains and other curtains which do not require much fullness may be made up with a simple casing which slots on to a narrow curtain rod or plastic covered spring wire.

Estimating fabric

The width of the curtain depends on the fullness required. This type of heading is not very suitable if a fullness of more than 1½ times the window width is required.

Allow 5cm (2in) for hems at each side and 1.5cm (½in) for each side of each seam if fabric widths are to be joined. For the heading, allow 12cm (5in) above the curtain rod.

For the hem, allow 10cm (4in).

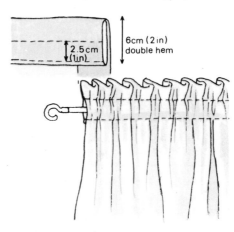

1. Curtain casing.

Making up

Join fabric widths as for unlined curtains. Make 2.5cm (1in) double hems (see Sewing Guide) down each side of the curtain. Turn up a 5cm (2in) double hem across the lower edge of the curtain, enclosing weights if desired.

Casing. At the top of the curtain, turn over and tack (baste) a 6cm (2in) double hem.

Stitch in place with two lines of top stitching, 2.5cm (1in) apart, and the same distance from the top of the curtain (Fig. 1). This produces a casing with a 2.5cm (1in) heading above the curtain rod. The proportions may be adjusted according to the shape and size of the window and the position of the curtain rod or wire.

TAPES

Curtain tapes are the easiest way to head a curtain. They are available in a wide range of sizes and colours, depending on specific needs. As has been said, they provide comparatively

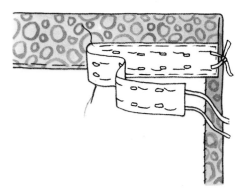

1. Pull cords out of ends of tape. Knot cords at one end. Turn under ends.

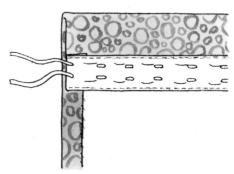

2. Sew tape to curtain, leaving cords free for gathering.

quick methods of gathering or pleating curtains and often contain slots for the curtain hooks.

For all styles, tack (baste) the tape in position and, before machine stitching, insert a few hooks. Try the curtain at the window to check that the tape is correctly placed, and adjust if necessary.

GATHERED HEADING

Tape for a gathered heading is about 2.5cm (1in) deep and is usually positioned about 2cm (just under 1in) from the top of the curtain. It is not stiffened, so for a crisper finish, stiffen the top 5cm (2in) of the curtain with a heavyweight dress interfacing, either iron-on or sewn in.

Fabric width. With a gathered tape, the curtain should be 1½-2 times the width of the track. The fullness can be distributed evenly across the area when the cords are drawn up. It is possible to get away with using the smaller amount of fabric if it is heavy, but use the full amount with a fine fabric or the curtain will look skimped.

Applying the tape. Cut tape 3cm (1¼in) longer than the finished flat curtain width. Pin, tack (baste) it across top of curtain (Fig. 1), leaving the ends free. Ease the cords out of the tape for the last 1.5cm (½in) at each end of the tape.

Tie one pair of ends in a knot (at the front edge) but leave the other pair free.

Stitch the tape in place, turning the ends in and stitching them down as well (Fig. 2).

Draw the free cords up so that all the fullness is at the front edge of the curtain and tie the cords so that they are the correct width and distribute the fullness evenly across the curtain. Do not cut off surplus cord.

PENCIL PLEATS

The tapes for pencil pleats (Fig. 1) are somewhat deeper than those for an ordinary gathered heading, and they give a more formal effect (Fig. 2).

Ensure that you have the right depth of heading and position the pockets according to whether or not you want the track to show when the curtains are closed.

Fabric width. Pencil-pleating tape takes $2\frac{1}{4}$–$2\frac{1}{2}$ times more fabric than the pleated width of the curtain.

Apply the pencil-pleat heading as described for gathered heading.

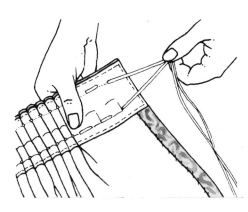

1. Draw up cords to make pencil pleats, distributing the gathers evenly.

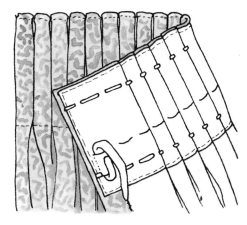

2. Pencil-pleated heading : some tapes have one row of slots, which can be positioned so that they are well down the heading (as shown) or at the top.

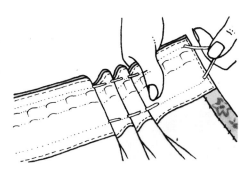

1a. Pinch pleats using drawstring tape.

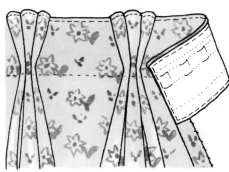

1b. The pleats are spaced evenly.

PINCH PLEATS

Pinch pleats may be made with two different types of tape.

Draw-string tape

This pleating tape has draw-strings, like the gathered and the pencil-pleating types. As you draw the strings up, three pleats, followed by a flat section are formed repeatedly along the top of the curtain (Figs. 1a and b). Pinch-pleat heading tapes may be quite deep (almost 10cm (4in) in some cases) and are usually quite stiff, so that extra stiffening is unnecessary.

Fabric width. The exact amount of fabric needed depends on the brand of tape, but 2–$2\frac{1}{4}$ times the width of the track is about right for triple pleats.

The tape is applied in the same way as pencil pleat tape, but it must be arranged so that the pleats are symmetrically placed.

Returns. If the window frame has a return on either side, the outer ends of the curtain should not be gathered. Attach the tape so that there is a single hook at the outer edge and the first pleat is at the *corner* of the return (Fig. 2).

The amount left unpleated at the centre of the curtains depends on the amount of overlap afforded by the track and fitments but the two central pleats should be the same distance apart as the pleats across the width of the curtain (Fig. 2b).

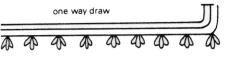

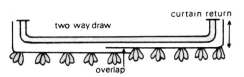

2. Position first pleat at track corner. Space overlap pleats evenly.

Slotted tape

The second type of pinch pleat tape has slots all along the length of the curtain into which pronged hooks are slotted (Fig. 3). Triple, double or single pleats may be formed by slotting 4, 3 or 2 prongs, as appropriate, into the fabric.

The prongs themselves are quite long and provide stiffening.

Fabric width. The amount of fabric needed depends on the brand of tape used, the spacing between the hooks and on whether you make single, double or triple pleats. Estimates range from $1\frac{3}{4}$ times the track length for single pleats to $2\frac{1}{4}$ times the track for triple pleats.

Apply the tape by stitching it to the curtain, turning under both ends.

Arrange the hooks so that there is a single pleat at each end and the remaining hooks are spaced evenly down the curtain (see Fig. 2).

Return. On curtains with a return round the sides of the window, arrange the pleats as described for draw-string pleated curtains.

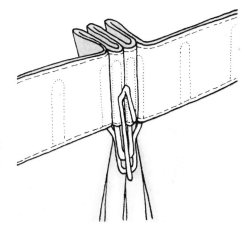

3. With a slotted tape and pronged hooks it is possible to vary the spacing.

HAND PLEATING

Hand pleating gives a professional finish to curtains, but it is, of course, more time-consuming.

The first step, with any of the following methods, is to stiffen the top 7.5–10cm (3–4in) of the curtain. Use a heavy-weight dressmaker's stiffening either ironed-on or sewn-in.

Cut a strip of interfacing 10cm (4in) wide to the length of the width of the finished flat curtain. Catchstitch or iron it to the wrong side 7.5cm (3in) below the top as shown below.

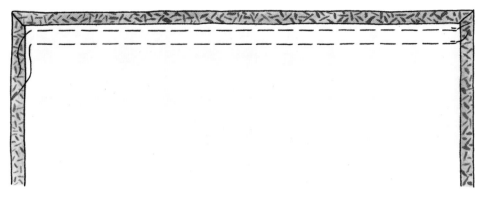

1. For a gathered heading make two rows of stitching across top of curtain.

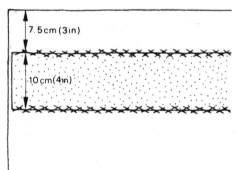

1. Apply interfacing to main fabric.

PENCIL PLEATS

Make up the curtain as described previously, allowing slightly more fullness than you would if using a pleating tape.

Stitching the heading. Stitch the heading on the wrong side of the fabric. Use a long length of button thread or sewing thread doubled. If you have to use more than one length of thread, double stitch where new thread joins so there is no gap in the pleating.

Make two rows of gathering stitches along the width of the curtain, positioning the two rows about 4cm (1½in) apart and matching exactly (Fig. 1). Make stitches about four times as long on the wrong side of the fabric as on the right side.

Pull up threads (Fig. 2) to desired width (the same length as the curtain track), and tie the ends.

Cut a piece of plain or pocketed (non draw-string) curtain tape 3cm (1¼in) longer than the width of the curtain and pin the tape across the top of the curtain. Oversew by hand, catching each pleat to the tape (Fig. 3).

Locking pleats. To give the heading greater depth, lock the pleats as shown in Fig. 4.

Hooks. Stitch hooks to the tape, or use spiked hooks. If the tape has pockets, use standard curtain hooks. Neaten ends of tape by oversewing.

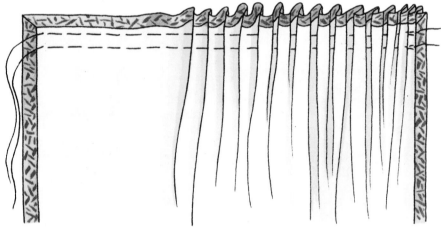

2. Draw up threads and tie ends securely. Space gathers evenly.

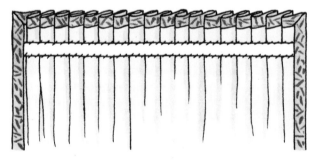

3. Stitch tape to curtain, anchoring each pleat firmly.

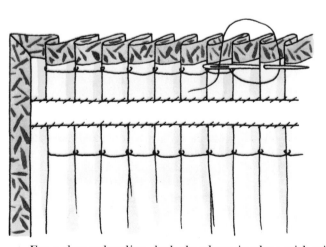

4. For a deeper heading, lock the pleats in place with stitching.

PINCH PLEATS

With careful calculation, it is possible to make pinch pleats to fit the rail exactly, positioning the pleats so that there is one at each end and they are evenly spaced along the track.

Fabric width. Generally, allow two to two and a half times the curtain track.

To calculate pleats, subtract from the made up flat curtain the heading width required. Remember to allow for return and overlap. The amount left over, *the spare amount*, is for pleats. Allow four pleats per width of fabric used i.e. if each curtain is $1\frac{1}{2}$ widths wide, allow six pleats. Then divide the spare amount by the number of pleats e.g. $1\frac{1}{2}$ widths = 6 pleats. Spare ÷ 6. *For spaces between pleats,* mark return at one end and overlap at front edge. Then divide the remainder of the finished width by the number of spaces, e.g. a 6 pleat ($1\frac{1}{2}$ width) curtain with a return at one end and an overlap at the other will have 5 spaces. If the pleated heading is 50cm ($\frac{1}{2}$yd) wide, this divided by 5 makes each space 10cm ($3\frac{3}{5}$ in).

Making up. Make up interfaced curtain and, using tailor's chalk, mark lines on the wrong side of the curtain at the calculated intervals (Fig. 1).

Join the first two marks with a vertical line of tacking stitches, then join the next two marks and continue making single pleats across top of the fabric.

Stitch these single pleats with a line of machine stitching 4cm ($1\frac{1}{2}$in) long, starting 6cm ($2\frac{1}{2}$in) from the top of the curtain (Fig. 2).

Tuck two folds of fabric inwards to make a triple pleat. Handstitch through the pleat at the base of the line of machine stitching to hold the pleat, using running stitch. For a soft effect, stop stitching 1cm ($\frac{1}{4}$in) from the front of the pleat (Fig. 3). Another method is to hold the pleats together by simply oversewing the front edges at point A (see Fig. 3).

It is not necessary to sew on a curtain tape. Hooks may be attached to the curtain itself. Position each hook at a pleat.

BOX PLEATS

Fabric width. For box pleats, allow three times the length of the track. The total width of the curtain should be divisible by 30cm (12in) since each pleat takes about 30cm (12in).

Making up. Mark the positions of the folds across the fabric. Make the first mark 5cm (2in) from the edge of the curtain and the next 5cm from that. Then mark alternately 10cm

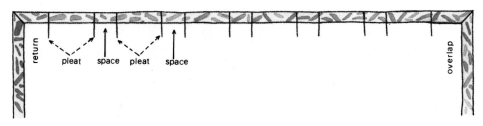

1. Mark position of pleats and spaces: allow four pleats per width.

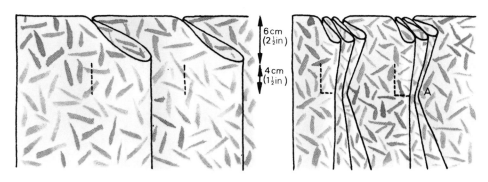

2. Stitch single pleats by machine. *3. Fold single pleats into triple pleats.*

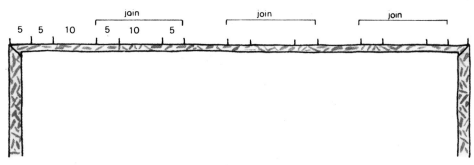

1. Mark the box pleat folds across fabric as shown and join pleats together as indicated.

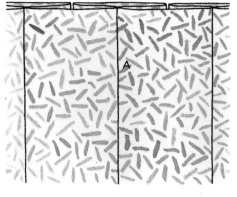

2. Flatten pleats as shown.

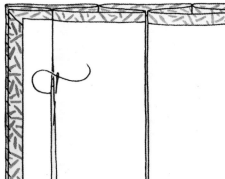

3. Slipstitch pleats at back.

(4in) and 5cm (2in) across the curtain, ending with two marks 5cm (2in) apart (Fig. 1).

Starting 20cm (8in) from one end, join this mark to the next one 20cm (8in) away. Pin, tack (baste).

Leave a 10cm (4in) space and join the next 20cm (8in) piece together. Repeat down the length of the curtain.

These pleats may be machine stitched.

Start 2cm ($\frac{3}{4}$in) from the top of the curtain and stitch down for 8cm ($3\frac{1}{4}$in). Then flatten the pleats (Fig. 2) and pin in position. Only the *front* pleats (point A) are stitched.

Next stitch the back of the pleats, using slipstitch. Stitch right through the lining to the main fabric to prevent sagging (Fig. 3).

Attach hooks to the curtain.

91

SCALLOPED HEADINGS

Scalloped headings are generally used on café curtains and involve a rather different technique in making up and finishing. Two of the most effective styles, Figs. 1 and 2, are plain scallops with the curtain ungathered, or pleated scallops like a pinch-pleated curtain. Both headings involve much the same technique, but the amount of fabric varies.

Estimating fabric

For plain scallops, the finished width of the curtain should be the same as the length of the curtain track. Allow 4cm, (1½in) at each side for hems. For the length of the curtain, add 1.5cm (½in) at the top and 10cm (4in) for the hem. Work out how many scallops will fit across the window. In this example the scallops will be 8cm (3¼in) wide, with a spacing of 2cm (¾in) between them (Fig. 3), so divide the width of the window by 10cm (4in) to find the number of scallops, add one to find the number of spaces (there will be a space at each end of the curtain).

For pleated curtains, multiply the number of spaces by 8cm (3¼in) to find how much fabric the pleats will take up. Add this figure to the total width of the curtain, plus the usual side hem allowances for the total width of fabric needed for the curtain.

Facing. The top of scalloped curtains has to be faced to give a neat finish round the curves.

Cut a 15cm (6in) strip of fabric (either the same as the curtain or in a plain lining material) to the same width as the curtain fabric.

Template

In order to cut the scallops to the same size, you will need a template of the size of the finished scallop. For these examples, cut it out of stiff card, following the measurements given (Fig. 4). The shape of the scallops is based on a circle, squared off at the top end.

Marking the positions. For plain scallops, on the wrong side of the fabric, starting 6cm (2¼in) from one end, mark out the shape of the scallop, leaving 2cm (¾in) between each curve (Fig. 5).

For the pleated curtains, again on the wrong side of the fabric, starting 13cm (5in) from one raw edge, mark out the shape of the scallop, leaving 10cm (4in) gaps between each of the scallops (Fig. 6).

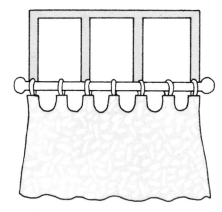

1. Plain scalloped heading.

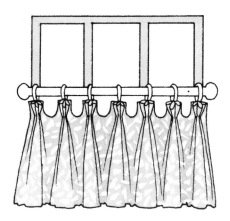

2. Scalloped heading with pleats.

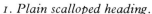
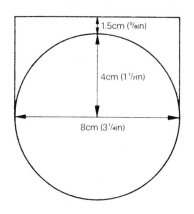

3. Measuring for a plain scalloped heading.

4. To make a template for the curtains shown, start by drawing a circle with a radius of 4cm (1½in).
Mark in the diameter horizontally.
Using a set square, mark in a rectangle with the diameter as one side, making the adjacent sides 5.5cm (2⅛in) for examples illustrated.
Cut out the template round the outer lines.

5. Mark the scallops across the width of the curtain.

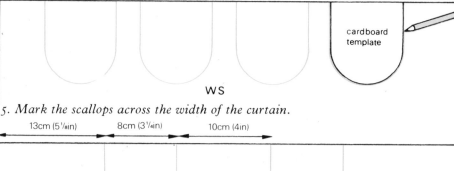

6. For pleated headings, allow more space between scallops.

Applying the facing

Turn up a 1cm ($\frac{1}{2}$in) double hem across the lower edge of the facing. Match the facing to the top of the curtain, with right sides together and tack (baste) in place across the top and bottom.

Mark a line between the scallops 1.5cm ($\frac{5}{8}$in) from the top of the curtain. Tack (baste) round the chalked lines, through both layers of fabric (Fig. 7). Machine stitch the facing to the curtain, starting from the bottom of the facing and stitching up the seamline at the side of the curtain (4cm ($1\frac{1}{2}$in) from the raw edge), stitching along the top and along the chalked lines round each curve as you come to it (Fig. 8).

Cut out the scallops, 5mm ($\frac{1}{4}$in) from the stitching.

Clip into the curves, Fig. 9.

Finishing

Stitch 2cm ($\frac{3}{4}$in) deep double hems down each side of the curtain, using slipstitch and clipping into the seam allowance of the curtain at the base of the facing.

Turn up the hem as for unlined curtains (page 85) and turn the faced section of the curtain right side out.

For plain scallops, attach a curtain ring in the centre of each scallop.

For pinch pleated curtains, mark two lines, 8cm ($3\frac{1}{4}$in) apart, each 1cm ($\frac{3}{8}$in) from the edge of a scallop. With wrong sides together, join these two lines by a 2cm ($\frac{3}{4}$in) line of stitching, starting 2cm ($\frac{3}{4}$in) from the top of the curtain.

Tuck two folds into the centre of the pleat to make a triple pleat and stitch as described for hand-made pinch pleat (Fig. 10).

Sew a ring to the top of the curtain, catching the centre pleats together (as in Fig. 2).

Fabric loops. For scalloped curtains hung from fabric loops, (the reverse of the roller blind edging on page 71) it is necessary to allow a longer strip of fabric between the scallops.

When cutting a template, instead of allowing only 1.5cm ($\frac{5}{8}$in) above the top of the circle, extend the straight sides by a further 10cm (4in). Make up the curtains and face the scallops as described above. Instead of stitching a ring to top of the scallop, turn under 5cm (2in) and stitch to the back of the faced curtain, to make a loop. The curtain rod can then be slotted on.

For castellated headings: use a rectangular template, 9.5cm by 8cm (4in by 3$\frac{1}{4}$in) rather than the curved template.

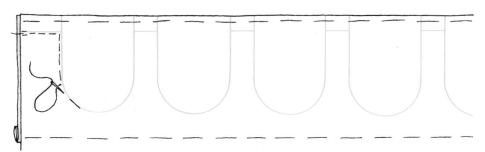

7. To face the scallops, tack facing to right side of curtain, following the marked outline of the scallop. Between the scallops, tack straight across 1.5cm ($\frac{5}{8}$in) from the raw edges.

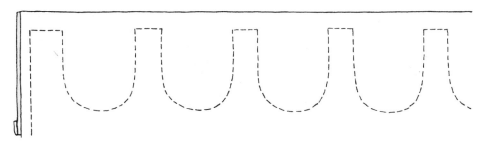

8. Machine stitch the facing in place.

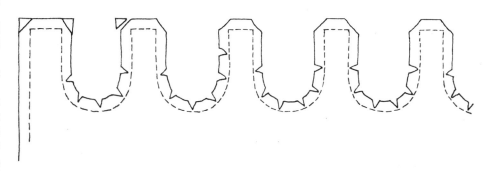

9. Cut out scallops 5mm ($\frac{1}{4}$in) from stitching. Notch the curves and clip the corners.

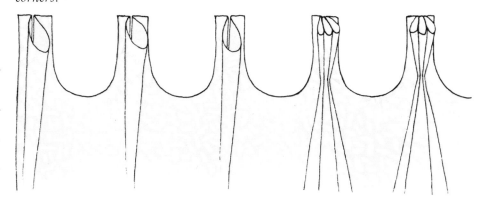

10. For pleated curtains, make a pleat in the middle of each of the spaces between the scallops, as described for handmade pinch-pleated headings.

93

Shower curtains

Shower curtains are made in a slightly different way to ordinary curtains. Stitching weakens the waterproof fabric, so they are made up with as little stitching as possible. Also, they do not need to be as full as curtains round beds or in windows.

Accessories

Shower curtains are usually fixed to a rail round the shower or along the bathtub. Special hooks are available which serve the double purpose of acting as runners and curtain hooks. They are fixed to the curtain through eyelet holes made with a special hole punch in the top hem of the curtain. Shower curtains should be stitched with a nylon or synthetic thread rather than with ordinary cotton. Use paper clips and adhesive tape rather than pins and lines of tacking (basting) to hold the fabric in place while it is being stitched.

When stitching plastic fabric, use a long loose stitch on the sewing machine. A little oil on the tip of the needle will make stitching easier – use the lubricant for your sewing machine.

Estimating fabric

The finished curtain may be up to 1½ times the width of the area to be screened, although fullness is not necessary.

Allow 5cm (2in) for each side hem and for the lower hem, and allow 8cm (3in) for the heading. Include the usual seam allowance if you need to join widths of fabric, and remember to calculate extra if matching a pattern.

Making up

Start by joining fabric widths if necessary. Use a French seam (see Sewing Guide) to keep the curtain watertight.

Turn in and stitch 2.5cm (1in) deep double hems down each side of the curtain and across the lower edge, mitring the corners (Fig. 1).

Turn over a 4cm (1½in) double hem at the top of the curtain, but do not stitch as this would weaken the fabric unnecessarily. Using a special punch, make metal-trimmed eyelet holes about 15cm (6in) apart across the top of the curtain, with one hole at each edge of the curtain.

If you do not have a punch, it is possible to use a standard heading tape – choose a nylon tape rather than a cotton one.

Insert the loop hooks into the holes and hang from a bar round the shower (Fig. 3).

1. Turn under and stitch double hems down sides and across lower edge.

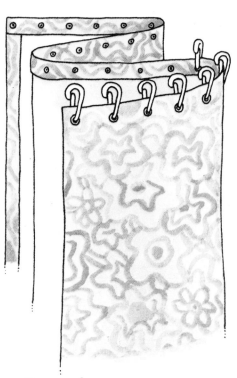

2. Turn under hem across upper edge, make eyelets through both thicknesses.

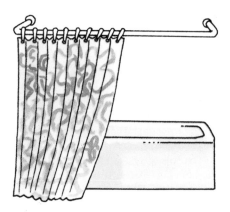

3. Shower curtains are hung from a rail round a bath or shower.

Tie - backs

Tie-backs are a useful method of holding bulky curtains clear of the window, to let in as much light as possible.

Measuring

To calculate the finished length of the tie-back, hold a tape-measure round the curtain to take in as much fullness as necessary (Fig. 1). Allow a couple of centimetres (about an inch) for attaching hooks to hold the tie-backs. Note the length of tape required and the position in which the hook should be.

Making up

The finished depth of the tie-back should be about 10cm (4in), but this may be varied to match the proportions of the curtains.

For each tie-back, cut two strips of fabric to the finished measurement of the tie-back, plus 1.5cm (½in) all round (Fig. 2).

Cut a piece of interfacing (and a piece of bump if extra body is needed) to the finished measurement of the tie-back. Tack (baste) interfacing (and bump if used) to the wrong side of one piece of the tie-back, positioning it centrally. Catchstitch in place (Fig. 3).

Position the second piece of fabric on the right side of the interfaced tie-back with wrong side upwards.

Pin, tack (baste) and stitch all round, leaving an opening 10cm (4in) long down one long side (Fig. 4). (If the fabric is very bulky – velvet or heavy brocade – use lining fabric rather than curtain fabric for this second piece.)

Grade seam allowances and clip corners.

Turn tie-back right side out and slipstitch closed down opening.

Attach a small ring to each end and screw a hook into the wall or window reveal (Fig. 5).

Shaped tie-backs

Tie-backs which curve upwards from the centre to the edges are a graceful variation. The lower edge may be scalloped, for example, or braid added for extra decoration.

Make a pattern of the desired shape, drawing it on folded paper of half the required length (Fig. 6) and placing the centre of the tie-back to the fold to ensure both halves are symmetrical.

Cut out the pattern, unfold it and try it round the pulled-back curtain.

Cut out both sides of the tie-back at the same time by placing the unfolded pattern on double fabric; remember to allow 1.5cm (½in) all round for turnings. Continue as for straight tie-backs.

1. Measure length required for tie-back.

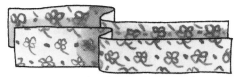

2. Cut two strips for each tie-back.

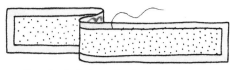

3. Catchstitch interfacing to wrong side of one piece of fabric.

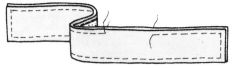

4. Right sides together, pin, tack and stitch the two pieces of fabric together.

5. Sew a ring at each end of tie-back.

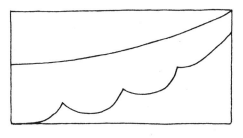

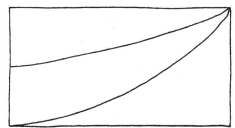

6. Draw half of shaped tie-backs on paper, add a seam allowance all round and then mark pattern on the fabric with tailor's chalk.

95

Pelmets and valances

Pelmets and valances are used to cover the top of the curtain, either to hide a track or heading, or for decoration or additional height. Pelmets are made of painted wood, or of fabric attached to a board fitted across the window reveal. Padded fabric pelmets applied directly to the board can also be made using upholstery techniques (see foam upholstering in chapter eight), but the method given here is for a stiffened fabric which is removable for cleaning. Valances are softer in effect than pelmets and usually consist of pleats or gathers attached to a rod or track projecting above the window.

The depth of a pelmet or a valance will depend on the size of the curtains, but 15 to 30cm (6 to 12in) is perhaps average.

PELMETS

The pelmet board may be made from plywood or hardboard painted to match the room, or covered in fabric to match the curtains. Pelmets sometimes have contours to add interest but it is not necessary to shape the pelmet board unless it is to be painted or upholstered. In the method described here, the stiffened fabric is shaped, then stretched across a board frame. A selection of pelmet shapes is shown below.

Fixing the pelmet board

The pelmet may be constructed in various ways, depending on the shape and size of the window and the style in which the curtains are hung.

Recessed curtains. The board may be attached to the window frame if the curtains are hung inside the reveal. In this case it is generally made of plywood 1cm ($\frac{1}{2}$in) thick and fixed in place with angle irons, screwed into the back of the board and to the upper surface of the reveal (Fig. 1).

Position the angle irons so that the pelmet board will lie flush with the inner edge of the beading of the window frame.

Projecting pelmet. The board may be attached to a shelf fixed above the window. In this case, the shelf and end pieces are made from plywood fixed to the wall with angle irons as shown in fig. 2 opposite.

The pelmet should project from the wall by about 10cm (4in) in order to leave sufficient clearance for the track fittings and the curtains which are bulkiest when pulled back.

Base the length of the pelmet on the track length, allowing an extra 2.5cm (1in) at each end for access when fitting the runners onto the track and for hanging the curtains.

The curtain track may be fixed to the

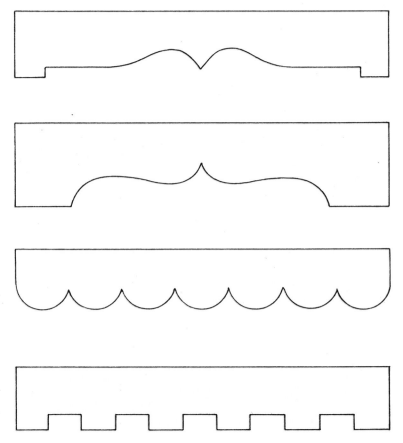

Differently shaped pelmets.

lower surface of the shelf or to the wall. The shelf is fixed with angle irons, spaced evenly down the length of the board, about 20cm (8in) apart. The wall above a window is often particularly hard, so attach the irons to the wall first, as drilling may be difficult. If there is a concrete lintel, it may be necessary to use a hammer action electric drill.

Calculate the positions for the bracket, mark the positions for the screws and drill the holes. Insert fibre or plastic wall plugs and fix the angle irons in place.

Fix the ends of the shelf in place by screwing them to the shelf piece (Fig. 3).

Rest the pelmet shelf on the angle irons and mark the positions of the screws. Remove the board and drill pilot holes in the wood, then screw in place (Fig. 4).

The pelmet board itself may be made of plywood or hardboard. Pre-shaped hardboard pelmets are available for pelmets where a painted finish is required. They have the advantage of being light and easy to fix – they are simply nailed to the front of the pelmet shelf. The board may, alternatively, be made from 1cm ($\frac{1}{2}$in) plywood, nailed or screwed in place before the pelmet shelf is finally fixed.

1. For a pelmet in the recess, screw angle irons to top of reveal.

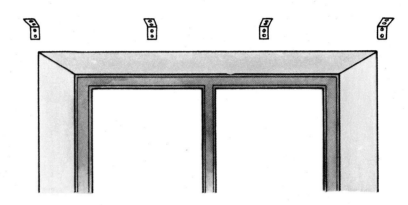

2. For a wall-fixed pelmet, attach angle irons to wall above window.

3. Fix end pieces to shelf for a crisp finish.

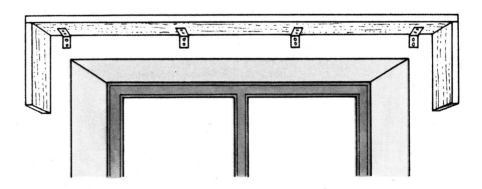

4. Fix shelf to the angle irons, centring it above the window.

Measuring and estimating

Measure the board to which the pelmet is to be attached, measuring round the corner if the pelmet projects. Choose a shape for the pelmet: straight, gently curved upwards, scalloped, castellated and so on.

Make a template from which to cut the fabric.

Cut a strip of paper a little larger than the desired size of the pelmet.

Fold the paper in half widthwise and draw out the shape of the pelmet on one half (Fig. 1).

Cut out the shape and try it for size and effect before cutting out the fabric.

You will need the following fabrics: a piece of buckram the same shape and size as the template, a piece of curtain fabric, a piece of lining and a piece of interlining 1.5cm ($\frac{1}{2}$in) larger all round than the template; also braid, trim or piping – according to taste.

Method

Lock the interlining to the wrong side of the curtain fabric as described on page 87.

Lay the pelmet fabric and interlining down flat with interlining side up.

Place the interfacing (buckram) in position over the interlining and tack (baste) round the edges, (Fig. 2).

Clip or notch the seam allowance, if necessary, and turn the border of fabric over the buckram (Fig. 3). Turn in a seam allowance on the lining fabric, clipping and notching as necessary.

If piping is to be added, stitch it to the back at this point (see the Sewing Guide for piping instructions).

Lay the lining on the buckram, right side up, and slipstitch in place, catching the lining to the seam allowance of the curtain fabric (Fig. 4).

If using a trimming, try it on the pelmet to establish the best position. Then slipstitch it on neatly by hand.

Fixing the pelmet

The pelmet may be fixed to the board in various ways. The simplest way is to tack it in place. The line of tacks may then be covered with braid trim glued in place with fabric glue (Fig. 5). If the pelmet is to be dry cleaned, there are two alternatives. Either attach curtain rings (Fig. 6) to the back of the pelmet, and hook them over small nails projecting from the pelmet board, or attach Velcro to the back of the pelmet and glue matching strips to the pelmet board.

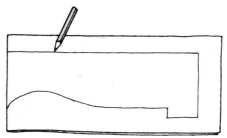

1. Cut a paper template for the pelmet.

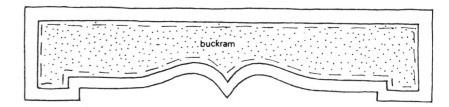

2. Stitch buckram to wrong side of interlined curtain fabric.

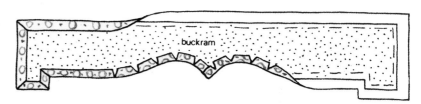

3. Clip seam allowances and turn over edge of buckram.

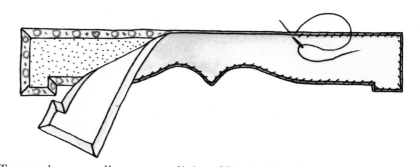

4. Turn under seam allowances on lining. Slipstitch in place.

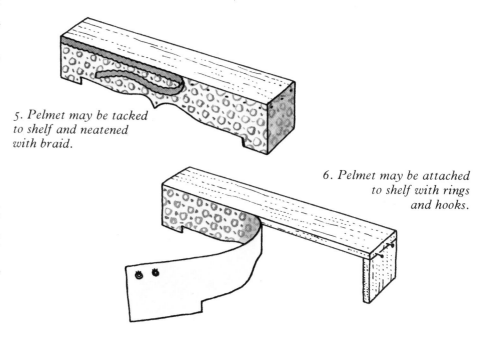

5. Pelmet may be tacked to shelf and neatened with braid.

6. Pelmet may be attached to shelf with rings and hooks.

VALANCES

Valances give a softer, less formal effect at the head of a curtain. They may be simply gathered, or any of the pleated headings described earlier can be used. However, it is important to stiffen the fabric before making the heading, and to position the tape 5cm (2in) from the top of the strip of fabric so that the valance will not sag.

Estimating fabric

Estimate the width of the fabric in the same way as for curtains, depending on the heading chosen. As with curtains, pleats may be made with a gathering or pleating tape, or by hand. The length of fabric needed is equal to the depth of the finished valance, plus a hem allowance of 4cm (1½in), plus a heading allowance of 7cm (3in).

Method

Cut fabric and lining to measurements, and cut a piece of interlining and a piece of interfacing to the finished measurement of the valance.
Stiffen the curtain fabric, positioning the stiffening material 7cm (3in) from the top of the strip for the valance.
Lock the interlining to the stiffened fabric, positioning it over the fabric as shown in Fig. 1.
Lock the lining to the interlining, leaving 14cm (6in) unstitched at the top and 8cm (3in) unstitched at the lower edge.
Turn in the allowances all round the valance and slipstitch the lining to the curtain fabric as described for locked-in linings.
Apply the curtain tape or make a hand-pleated heading as described earlier.

Mounting

Screw eyelet rings into the pelmet shelf above the window, positioning them every 5cm (2in) (Fig. 2).
Attach curtain hooks to the tape or hand-sewn heading on the valance, positioning the hooks to match the rings on the pelmet board. The valance can then be hooked on to the rings, and easily removed for dry-cleaning.

Cased heading

It is also possible to make a simple cased heading round the valance, and thread it on to a bar or rod projecting round the top of the curtain (Fig. 3). This type of valance does not need stiffening or interlining, and it need not even be lined. Make up as described for cased headings on page 88.

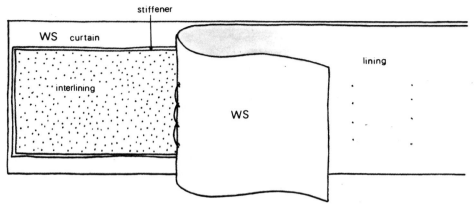

1. Lock the lining to the interlining.

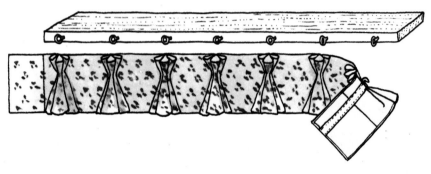

2. A valance with a curtain tape can be attached to the shelf with curtain hooks through eyelets.

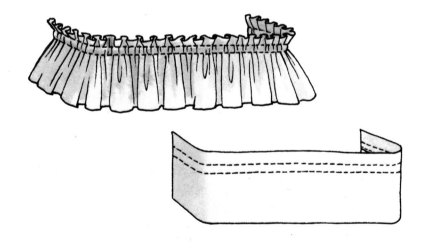

3. Valances may be slotted onto a metal track. Choose a full or a plain valance to match the décor.

99

These luxurious bed curtains are an excellent illustration of different headings and edgings. The main curtains are pencil pleated and a printed fabric is used for the lining which is visible inside the bed.
The valance heading is gathered and the same lining is used as on the main curtains.
Gathered curtains also cover the walls of this room and are attached by casing rods at top and bottom to hold them in position on the wall (see page 141).

Small things

Soft furnishings are normally thought of as things which play a major part in décor, requiring considerable commitment and considerable fabric. But as well as curtains, loosecovers, tablecloths and the like, there are a number of small things which can be made of furnishing fabrics and which have useful and decorative roles in the home. Several of them are illustrated in this chapter; all involve very simple techniques, minimum amounts of fabric and comparatively little labour. Some, such as the sponge bags and jewellery cases shown opposite use basic quilting designs (described earlier in this book), and most are decorated with ordinary bias binding trim.

FABRICS
Although several different fabrics could be used to make the items described here, cotton is probably the best and most economic material to use. In all cases, a washable fabric is recommended.

For linings, nylon ciré is suggested if waterproofing is needed. Otherwise, use an ordinary washable lining fabric or a lining made from the same fabric as the item itself.

METHOD
Most of the objects featured here are made from rectangles of cloth which, cut in different sizes and joined in different ways, give amazingly different results. For this reason, the chapter also serves as inspiration for imaginative use of fabric and thread. By thinking first of the item to be made, then reducing it to its essential elements and basic shape, new ideas emerge.

Size. Most of the articles described here, particularly the bags, can be made to any size. The patterns are on a graph and can therefore be enlarged to suit personal tastes and needs. A drawstring sponge bag can become a huge laundry bag by simply drawing the pattern to size and cutting out. Equally, a shoebag can be reduced to a fraction of its size and used to store earrings and jewellery.

Trimming. The bias binding used to trim most of the objects can be bought from haberdashers, either in matching or contrasting colours. The method of applying bias binding is described on page 148 in the Sewing Guide.

To use bias binding to make ties, as in the flap bags opposite, simply cut the desired length and stitch a seam along creased edges to hold them together.

BAGS

These four bags are made by sandwiching 2oz terylene wadding between nylon ciré (lightweight shower curtaining could be used instead) and the chosen fabric, then stitching with a simple quilting design (see pages 30–33).

Ready-made quilting can be used but it must be lined first with waterproof material if used for sponge bags.

The amount of fabric required depends on the size of the bag and although suggested sizes are given, bags can be made larger or smaller by enlarging the graph to suit.

Drawstring bag

As well as fabric, you will need cord for casing and bias binding for top edge.

Cut out as in Fig. 1. Plan shows two bags, one large, one small, cut from previously quilted fabric.

Following Fig. 2, make two rows of stitching 3.5cm (1⅜in) and 5cm (2in) from top edge of rectangle, to form draw-string casing.

Unpick vertical stitches of quilting between these rows to clear draw-string casing.

Join short edges of rectangle with French seam to form tube and bias bind top edge (see Sewing Guide).

Attach square base with French seam, beginning with *right sides together* so that the finished seam shows on outside (Fig. 3).

Make small openings in casing, either side of seam. Insert cord and tie knot at each end.

Pouch

You will need fabric plus 3m (3yd) of bias binding to make ties and 2.5m (2½yd) for pocket edging.

Cut out as in Fig. 1, one main piece and five pocket pieces.

Following Fig. 2, bias bind tops of small pocket sections, stitching a 15cm (6in) tie in the centre of front pocket.

Then stitch pocket sections together in pairs, wrong sides together, along curved edge. Stitch fifth section to main piece.

Bias bind round curved edges of pockets, stitching a tie at centre top and bottom of main piece (Fig. 3).

Add 1m (1yd) loops on either side (Fig. 3).

Join pockets by stitching 10cm (4in) at A and B, including a 15cm (6in) tie at A at the same time.

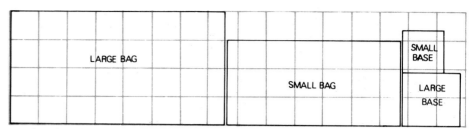

1. Cutting plan for two bags. One square = 7.5cm (3in).

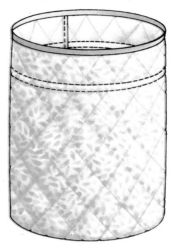 

2. Work two rows of stitching round top of fabric to form a casing for the draw string. Unpick quilting within casing area. Join sides with French seam.

3. Join square base to main section with French seam on outside. Insert drawstring through holes in casing.

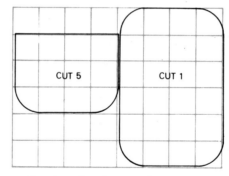

CUT 5   CUT 1

1. Cutting plan for pouch. One square = 7.5cm (3in).

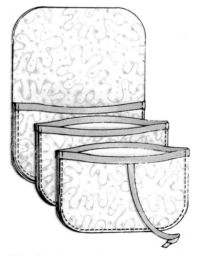 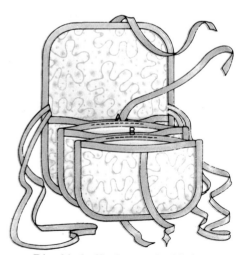

2. Bias bind tops of small pocket sections, sew curved edges together.

3. Bias bind all edges and add ties. Join pocket sections at A and B.

Bag with flap

You will need 3.5m (4yd) of bias binding plus fabric to fit bag size.

Cut out as in Fig. 1.

Bind both short edges of inside pocket. Place it on main section, wrong sides together (Fig. 2), making sure pocket piece is 2.5cm (1in) from bottom edge of main section.

Stitch pieces together down sides, 5mm ($\frac{1}{4}$in) in from edge. Bias bind all round.

Bind round edges of gussets (Fig. 3) and tack (baste) and stitch into sides of bag, wrong sides together. Start from point A and stitch through bound edges (Fig. 4).

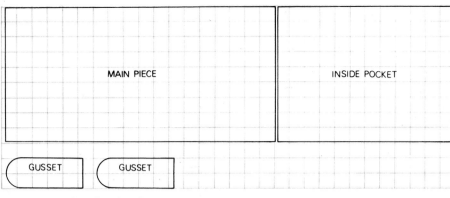

1. Cutting plan for flap bag.
One square = 4cm ($1\frac{1}{2}$in).

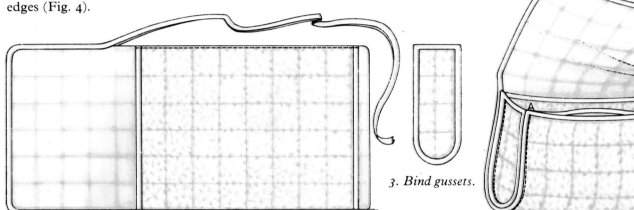

2. Position pocket, stitch sides down and bind edge.

3. Bind gussets.

4. Stitch gussets in. Start at point A.

Zip pocket bag

You will need fabric, bias binding and a 25cm (10in) zip.

Cut out as in Fig. 1.

Stitch zip along its lower edge, face down on to wrong side of main piece 1cm ($\frac{1}{2}$in) from top. Fold zip back as indicated in Fig. 2.

Bias bind edge of main piece, including over both zip tape ends at A and the stitched down one at B.

Bias bind both pocket pieces.

Stitch free edge of zip to inside top edge of small pocket section, concealing teeth as shown (Fig. 2). Neaten open end of zip.

Position pockets on main piece, wrong sides together. At centre sides of main piece and at zip ends, stitch 20cm (8in) ties.

Stitch round sides and lower edges of the pockets, sewing through both layers and keeping on the inner side of the bias binding.

Stitch up through the centre of large pocket to divide it into two sections (Fig. 3). Fold and tie bows to close.

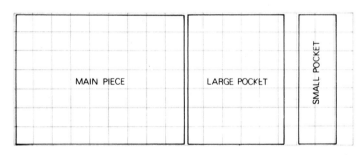

1. Cutting plan for zip pocket bag. One square = 4cm ($1\frac{1}{2}$in).

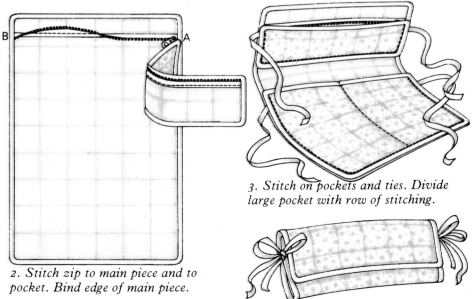

2. Stitch zip to main piece and to pocket. Bind edge of main piece.

3. Stitch on pockets and ties. Divide large pocket with row of stitching.

BASKET LININGS

Method 1 is for baskets with sloping sides.

You will need fabric 7.5cm (3in) deeper than basket, and enough to wrap round it twice, plus 3m (3yd) of bias binding.

Stand basket on fabric, draw round base and cut out shape (Fig. 1).

Measure around basket at widest circumference and add half as much again. Measure depth of basket and add 6cm (2½in).

Cut rectangle to these dimensions and join its short edges with a flat seam.

Following Fig. 2, pleat or gather fabric evenly to fit base circumference. Tack (baste) pleats to fabric base, right sides together; stitch with 1cm (⅜in) seam and trim to 0.5cm (¼in), then overcast edge.

If the basket has handles, cut and bias bind slits to accommodate them.

Make 1.5cm (⅝in) hem at top.

Fit lining and slot binding tape through hem, tying bow.

Method 2 is for basket with open weave top edge and straight sides.

You will need enough fabric to cover base and twice the depth of the basket, plus 2.5cm (1in) seam allowance × circumference + 2.5cm (1in). Stand basket on fabric, draw round base and cut out shape (Fig. 3).

Cut out rectangle.

Join short ends, right sides together, with flat seam; press. Fold over lengthwise to make double thickness, wrong sides together. Press, fold and stitch sides on to base, right sides together, with 1cm (⅜in) seam allowance (Fig. 4). Trim to 0.5cm (¼in), clip or pink and overcast edge.

Stitch four ties at top edge (see Fig. 4). Make stitch parallel to lining edge so that ties will tie properly.

Position lining and tie bows to basket.

Method 3 is for basket with sloping sides and open weave top and base.

You will need fabric for two circles with diameter A to B plus 2.5cm (1in) (Fig. 5) and six ties.

Cut out circles and ties. Fold ties in half and position at equal intervals round circumference of right side of one fabric circle, with loose ends inwards.

Stitch tie folds 0.5cm (¼in) from edge. Lay other fabric circle on top, right sides facing.

Tack, stitch around circle 1cm (½in) from edge, leaving a 10cm (4in) gap. Turn and slipstitch opening.

Centre lining in basket. Stab stitch through to its base. Tie ribbons to open weave edge at equal intervals.

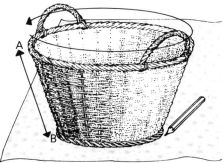

1. Draw round base of basket, marking fabric. For lining for sides, measure 1½ circumference × depth and add seam and hem allowances.

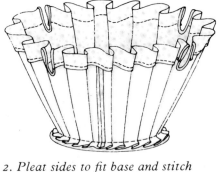

2. Pleat sides to fit base and stitch fabric pieces together. Make slots for handles, bind, stitch top hem.

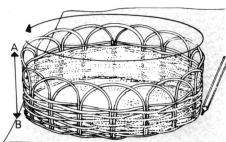

3. Draw round basket, marking fabric. Cut fabric twice circumference × 2AB + seam allowances.

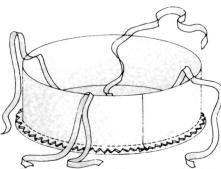

4. For sides, make side seam and fold fabric double. Stitch fabric to base and add ties as shown.

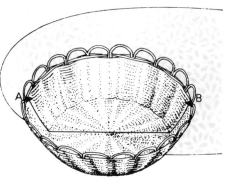

5. Cut two circles with A to B diameters, plus seam allowances.

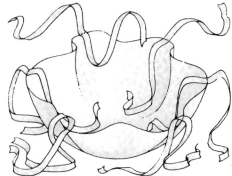

6. Sew fabric circles together, right sides facing, adding ties.

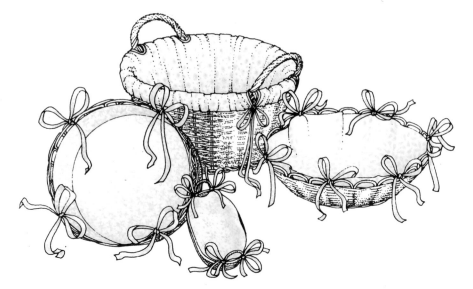

SHOEBAG

This can be made with or without a waterproof lining. You will need fabric of the dimensions given, plus batten rod and bias binding tape.

Cut out fabric and lining rectangles 47cm × 56cm (19½in × 22in) for the base, plus two 72cm × 18cm (28½in × 7in) strips for shoe pockets, and a fabric strip 47cm × 6cm (18½ × 2½in) for top border.

Tack (baste) and stitch main piece of fabric and lining, wrong sides together, 5cm (¼in) in from edge. Trim round fraying edges very slightly to make them even.

Using tailor's chalk, draw on main fabric the divisions shown in Fig. 1.

Tack (baste) and stitch the lining and fabric strips together (wrong sides facing) to make the two pocket strips. Bias bind the tops.

Following Fig. 2, divide pocket strips evenly between drawn vertical lines on main fabric. Tack (baste) and stitch along all drawn lines, then top-stitch with a close zigzag or apply bias binding along middle three lines.

Following Fig. 3, form pleats at pocket corners by pinning 2cm (¾in) in from pocket corners. Position side pleats 1cm (⅜in) from edge and centre ones slightly apart to show vertical divisions.

Tack (baste) carefully along bottom of pocket rows, then stitch 3mm (⅛in) from raw edge. Trim frayed edges and over stitch with close zigzag or apply bias binding strips.

Trim outer edges of shoe bag with bias binding, sandwiching in the outer edges of the pockets (Fig. 4).

For hanging loops make tape from bias binding 38cm (15in) long and cut into five equal pieces. Fold these into loops.

Press hems around remaining fabric strip, making it the exact width of the shoe bag. This is the batten casing.

Lay top edge of batten casing (right side) on top *back* edge of shoebag, sandwiching in loops positioned at the top of the vertical rows (Fig. 5). Tack and stitch.

Fold batten casing over to the right side and hem.

Topstitch with close zigzag.

Insert batten and hang bag by loops on hooks or on a pole.

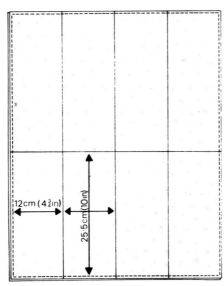

1. Using tailor's chalk, divide backing into sections as illustrated.

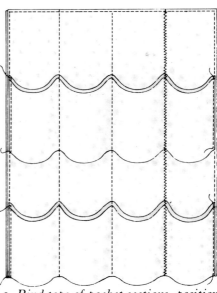

2. Bind tops of pocket sections, position on backing, spacing fabric evenly.

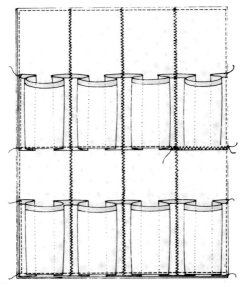

3. Pleat pocket excess and stitch down.

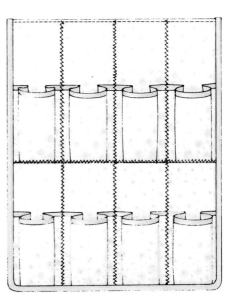

4. Top-stitch, then bind outer edge.

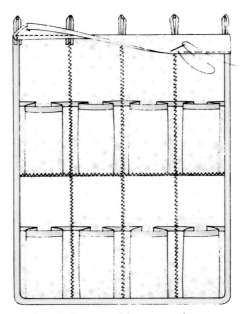

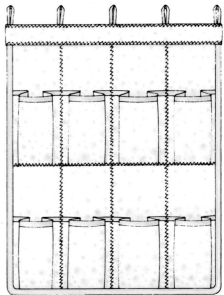

5. Attach loops and batten casing.

COATHANGER

You will need a wooden coathanger, wadding and fabric of the dimensions given.

Cut a strip of fabric 7.5cm (3in) longer than the hanger and 14cm (5½in) deep (Fig. 1).

Fold in half lengthwise, right sides facing. Draw a semi-circle 1cm (⅜in) in from either end, between the fold and the top 1.5cm (½in) seam allowance (Fig. 2).

Stitch along the curved lines, trim back to 5mm (¼in) and turn right side out. Press under seam allowance.

Wind coathanger with wadding until it is evenly fat and squashy with plenty of padding at both ends. The loose, springy wadding should have a circumference of around 15cm (6in) (Fig. 3).

Fit on the casing, pushing wadding well into the ends.

Nip the folded seam allowance together to firm down the wadding, then tack (baste) these edges together.

Finish with a running stitch in strong thread or embroidery cotton (Fig. 4). Tie a satin bow round the neck of the hanger.

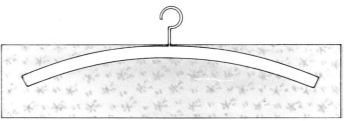

1. Cut cloth 14cm (5½in) deep and 7.5cm (3in) longer than hanger.

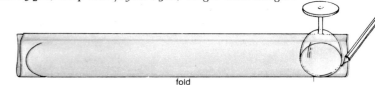

2. Fold fabric lengthwise and draw semi-circles at both ends.

3. Wrap hanger with wadding, tease into shape, padding ends well.

4. Fit cover, tack top, then stitch with running stitch.

TISSUE BOX

You will need enough fabric to wrap up a tissue box with a double layer, like a parcel, and four 18cm (7in) lengths of 1cm (⅜in) ribbon (these can be made from the same fabric or bought).

With the fabric doubled, mark a rectangle measuring A – B × the longer edge measurement of the box and another rectangle measuring C – D × the shorter edge measurement of the box.

Cut out, allowing 1.5cm (½in) seam allowance around each side. Lay one of the larger rectangles right side up and place the ribbons on the short edges so they are about 2.5cm (1in) from the corners and point inwards.

Lay the matching piece of fabric right side down on top and stitch round the edges, taking 1.5cm (½in) turnings; leave an opening in one side.

Turn right side out, fold in the seam turnings and slipstitch together.

Stitch the other rectangle in the same way.

Centre one rectangle on top of the other to form a cross (Fig. 2). Tack (baste) and topstitch together.

Decorate round the edges with open zigzag or an embroidery stitch.

Wrap up the box like a parcel, tying the bows on each side.

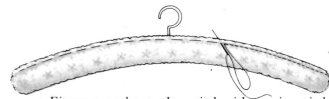

1. Measure sides of box, A to B, C to D.

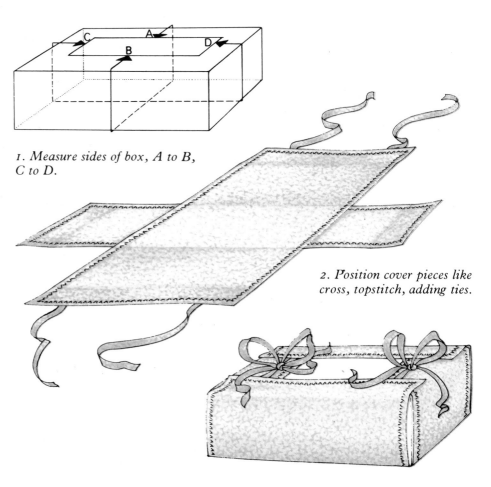

2. Position cover pieces like cross, topstitch, adding ties.

The articles shown here have several things in common. Basically they are all made of rectangles, yet by different treatments – gluing, lining, wrapping – they assume very different uses and appearances. Trimmings consist of bias binding and zigzag stitching, while the mirror frame has a pretty design painted on the printed fabric.

BOOK COVER

This method is suitable for covering notepads, address books etc. which already have hard covers.

You will need a rectangle of fabric the length × the open width of the book plus 5cm (2in) on each measurement, and white rubber or PVA-type glue.

Following Fig. 1, lay the book down on the wrong side of the fabric and draw round the front; roll to spine, mark spine, then roll to back and mark back (Alternatively, make a paper pattern in the same way first).

Draw 2.5cm (1in) margin beyond this and cut out the rectangle (Fig. 2).

Apply glue with a flat spreader or piece of cardboard to the front cover of the book (Fig. 3).

Position book face down on appropriate area of fabric, then turn over and place the spine of the book along the edge of a table and gently smooth fabric into crevice near spine edge and outwards from the centre (Fig. 4).

Apply glue to the spine as in Fig. 5 and glue the fabric down, smoothing it outwards (Fig. 6).

Turn book over, front cover down, apply adhesive to back (Fig. 7) and smooth fabric outwards (Fig. 8).

Make two slits from edge of fabric to both edges of book spine (Fig. 9), trim section between slits to 1.5cm (½in) and apply glue to wrong side. With the end of a pencil tuck into hollow of spine and smooth down (Figs. 10 and 11).

Trim diagonally across margin corners to within 5mm (¼in) of book corner (Fig. 12). Apply glue sparingly to front cover margins.

Fold margins on to book, taking care to keep the corners neat (Fig. 13).

Do the same with back cover.

Slip a sheet of clean waste paper between first and second pages and apply glue sparingly all over page one (endpaper) (Fig. 14).

Stick page to front cover, keeping book open and press down.

Repeat for back cover.

Rub off any excess glue and place book between clean papers under an evenly weighted board for two days until glue is completely dry.

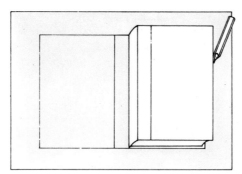

1. Mark the cover fabric by drawing round book edges.

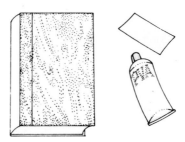

2. Allow a margin all round, then cut out the fabric.

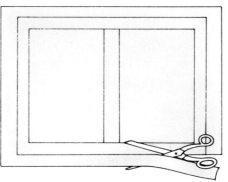

3. Spread glue over front cover.

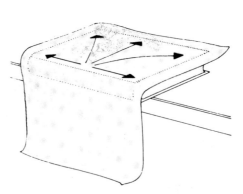

4. Smooth fabric over front cover.

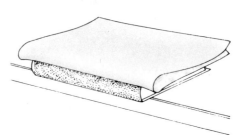

5. Fold fabric back and apply glue to book spine.

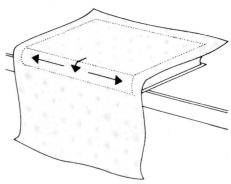

6. Smooth fabric over spine.

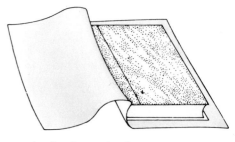

7. Apply glue to back cover.

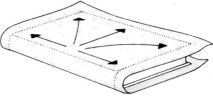

8. Smooth fabric over back cover.

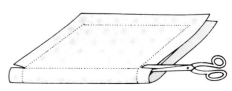

9. Cut slits in margins at spine.

10. Apply glue to trimmed margin.

11. Open book, tuck margins into spine and press down.

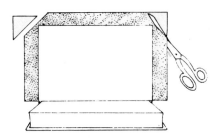

12. Trim margins diagonally at corners before folding down.

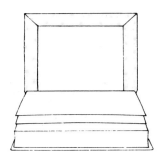

13. Stick margins inside covers.

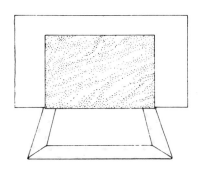

14. Apply glue over first page (endpaper) and stick it to inside cover.

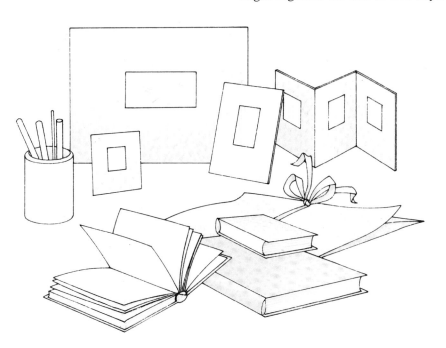

FRAME

You will need a mirror or, for a picture, framing glass or perspex just larger than picture; fabric and heavy cardboard, fabric glue and two curtain rings.

Cut two cardboard rectangles approximately double the length and width of the mirror or picture to be framed.

Cut two rectangles in fabric 5cm (2in) larger than cardboard.

Cut out a hole slightly smaller than the picture (mirror) in the middle of one cardboard piece. This is the frame front.

Cut a hole in one piece of fabric 1.5cm ($\frac{1}{2}$in) smaller each way than the hole in the frame front (Fig. 1).

Apply fabric glue evenly over one side of the cardboard front and lay it, sticky side down, on the wrong side of the fabric. Turn the fabric over and smooth it over the card.

Trim outer corners of fabric and stick outer edges down (see Fig. 1). Clip into the corners of the fabric in the hole, apply glue along margins and fold down over card.

A sheet of glass or perspex, 2.5cm (1in) larger all round than the hole may be secured behind opening with strong adhesive tape. Tape picture behind glass.

Sew the rings for hanging the picture in place on the right side of the backing fabric (Fig. 2). Stick the fabric to the card (Fig. 3), as described above. Apply glue to outer 5cm (2in) of frame front and back, being careful to avoid spoiling edge, (Fig. 4). Glue, then slipstitch front and back together.

Cover with clean paper and weight all edges together for one or two days.

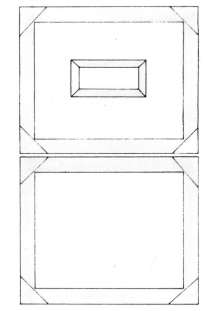

1. Cut out fabric and cardboard rectangles, as shown.

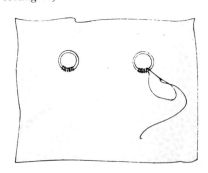

2. Sew rings to backing fabric.

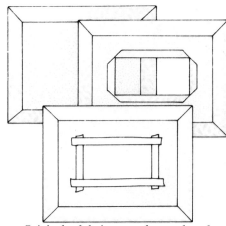

3. Stick the fabric over the card and turn back the edges.

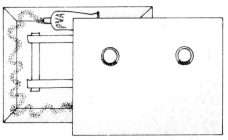

4. Stick frame front to frame backing and slipstitch outer edges together.

Loose covers may be fitted over the permanent upholstery covers of most styles of armchair or sofa and are, of course, removable for cleaning or repair. Loose covers are a good way of extending the life of permanent, or 'tight' covers, or of changing a colour scheme; but they should not be used as a cheap form of re-upholstery because they will not disguise sagging springs or lumpy padding.

As a rule, loose covers are made in sections which correspond to those on the original upholstery cover (the main exception to this is on scroll arms, described later on). Various paper patterns are on the market which serve as general cutting out guides for loose covers but the proper way to make a loose cover is to cut rectangles of fabric to fit the *overall* dimensions of each section of a chair or sofa, and then shape them by pinning them together on the piece of furniture. This is not difficult and the finished cover fits better than if a paper pattern is used.

Tuck-in. Fabric allowances are added to appropriate edges of the section rectangles so that they can be tucked into the crevices round the seat to anchor the cover and help prevent strain.

The bottom edge of the cover may be made with flaps which tie underneath for a plain finish. Alternatively, a skirt with corner kick pleats, or a gathered flounce can be made.

Piping the seams helps to prevent strain and forms a break between sections where it is not possible to match the pattern. It may be made in the same fabric as the cover or in a contrasting fabric.

The piping is applied to all main exposed seams, i.e. round the outside and inside back, outside and inside arms, border, cushions, bottom edge or between the bottom edge and skirt.

Note. There are many different styles of armchair and sofa and the instructions in this chapter should be regarded as a guide which can be adapted to suit individual needs. If your cover is very different from the example used here, it is wise to go to a shop and look at a similar one. Note the differences in construction, then incorporate them into the method described here.

Mint green covers give this room its brightness. The covers are made by cutting out rectangles of fabric and pinning them to the upholstery cover of each section and to each other.

FABRIC

Fabrics for loose covers should be tough and firmly woven for maximum wear - and colourfast and non-shrinkable if they are to be washed. There are many specially made furnishing fabrics in cotton, linen union and twill, and a light-weight upholstery fabric could also be used. Avoid anything thick or heavy as it is difficult to sew, particularly with piped seams where as many as eight layers of fabric may have to be fed through the machine.

Buy the best quality cloth you can afford: an average armchair uses 5-7m (6-8yd) and will take some time to make, so it is hardly worth while repeating the expense and effort too soon because a poor-quality cloth was used.

It is also essential to take time in measuring and estimating the amount of fabric required so that exactly the right amount is bought - this planning will also help when the fabric is cut out. Plain fabrics or small all over patterns are the easiest to work with and have a minimum of wastage.

Large patterns are more difficult as they have to be cut out carefully so that motifs are centred on the various sections of the cover, which inevitably involves wastage. If possible, check the size of the pattern repeat before you calculate the quantity required; with some very difficult patterns, particularly with expensive fabric, it may be worth buying a small piece first so that the cutting layout can be worked out with it in hand.

ACCESSORIES

Thread. Use regular sewing thread and allow two or three reels.

Piping cord. For piping, buy a medium-weight cord (No. 3 or 5), calculating the amount by measuring the edges to which it is to be applied and adding 50cm ($\frac{1}{2}$yd) for shrinkage. Wash and dry cord before using to ensure it is pre-shrunk.

Fastenings. The back opening may be finished with a heavy-duty zip fastener, touch-and-close tape or hooks and eyes. Hooks and eyes are described here as they are the easiest to apply, but instructions for applying zip fasteners appear in the Sewing Guide.

Miscellaneous. A sharp pair of cutting out scissors is essential; you will also need a fabric tape measure, graph paper, glass-headed pins, a piping foot for the sewing machine, a heavy duty machine needle and tailor's chalk.

Loose covers

MEASURING AND ESTIMATING

The different sections of sofas and armchairs have special names and these are given in Fig. 1. The rectangles of cloth which will be eventually shaped to fit the furniture are cut out first to cover these different sections.

Cushions. Remove any seat and back cushions and measure them as described on page 39 in the cushion chapter.

Measure the chair or sofa at the widest and the longest points of the sections; these are indicated by arrows in Fig. 2.

Add 3cm (1in) to each measurement for 1.5cm (½in) seam turnings and a further 15cm (6in) for tuck-ins at 1) the bottom and sides of the inside back, 2) the back and bottom of the inside arms and 3) back and sides of seat.

For a tailored skirt with kick pleats (Fig. 3a), subtract 15cm (6in) from the length measurement of the outside back and arms, front arms and border when measured from top to floor.

For a plain edge along the bottom (Fig. 3b), which ties underneath, measure each side of the chair or sofa along the bottom edge.

Allow enough fabric to cut four strips, 10cm (4in) deep by the measurement of each side *between the legs*. (You may find that you can cut these pieces from spare fabric.) The pieces will be sewn underneath later on.

Measure the width of each of the four sides of the chair or sofa 15cm (6in) above the floor, and allow pieces of fabric of these widths plus 18cm (7in) × 18cm (7in) deep.

For the insert pieces of the corner pleats allow four pieces 18cm (7in) square. (Lining and interfacing are optional.)

For a flounce (Fig. 3c) measure as for a tailored skirt, but allow enough fabric to make a strip 18cm (7in) deep by 1½ times the total perimeter of the piece of furniture.

Sofas. Loose covers for sofas are made in the same way as for chairs except that the fabric must be joined to make pieces wide enough for the outside and inside back and the front border. If there are seat cushions, position the seam in line with these throughout (Fig. 4a) – if by doing this you cannot match the pattern, incorporate piping in the seams.

If there are no seat cushions or if the sofa also has back cushions, use a whole fabric width as a centre panel and join pieces to each side to make up the width (Fig. 4b). Match the pattern carefully and do not include piping.

Aim for a continuity of pattern from the inside back, across the seat and down the front border.

Centre prominent motifs on the sections, excluding the tuck-in allowances. Join these sections before fitting the cover on the sofa.

Estimating main fabric

The most accurate way of estimating the amount of fabric needed overall is to make a cutting chart to scale. It is quite simple to do and will also help in cutting out.

Using graph paper in which one small square represents 10mm or ½in, draw rectangles to scale to represent each section of the cover (Fig. 5a).

Label the sections with names and dimensions, and cut them out of the paper.

On another sheet of paper, draw an open-ended rectangle in the same scale to represent the width of fabric.

For plain fabrics, arrange the small rectangles closely on the large one with all the length measurements parallel to the vertical edges.

For patterned fabrics, mark the length of the pattern repeat or the position of the main motif on the layout and place the small rectangles on it appropriately, remembering that the motifs should be centred on the part of the section that shows, rather than the whole area (Fig. 5b).

Piping fabric. Spare fabric can be used for the piping casing or, if there is no spare, add about 1m (1yd) for piping on chairs and 2m (2¼yd) for sofas.

Total. Measure the length of the layout and convert back in scale to give the total amount of fabric required.

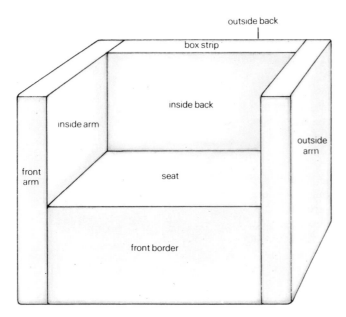

1. *Box-armed chair with seat cushion removed, showing the names of the sections. These apply to most styles.*

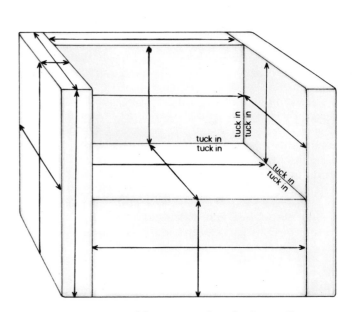

2. *Measure sections horizontally and vertically at longest and widest points, adding seam and tuck-in allowances.*

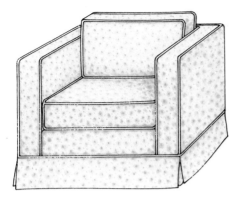

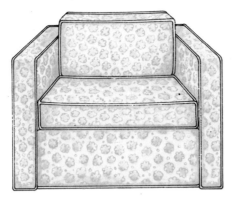

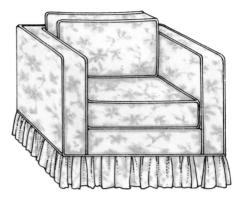

3a. *For a tailored skirt, subtract skirt length from pieces to which it is sewn.*

3b. *Plain hem has strips sewn to bottom edge and tied underneath.*

Gathered flounce gives informal finish. Subtract length as in 3a.

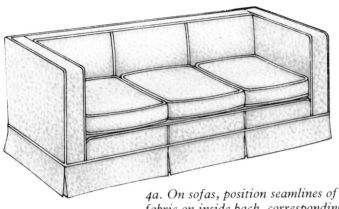

4a. *On sofas, position seamlines of fabric on inside back, corresponding with edges of seat cushions. Pipe seams when patterns do not match.*

4b. *Where there are no seat cushions, use whole width of fabric in central panel with narrow panels on each side.*

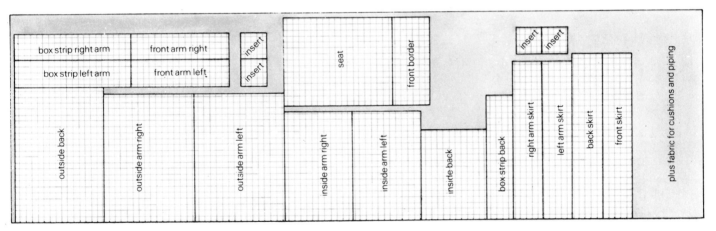

5a. *A typical cutting plan for plain fabric. All length measurements are parallel to selvedges.*

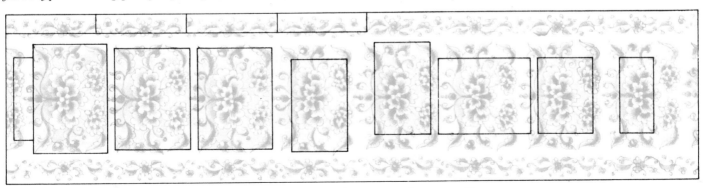

5b. *More complicated plan for large-patterned fabric, with pieces centred over motifs.*

CUTTING OUT

Cut out each section on the straight grain, following the layout and remembering to cut two outside and two inside arm sections. Label the pieces for easy identification.

FITTING THE COVER

A box-armed chair with a tailored skirt is used here to illustrate the fitting technique. Note, for example, that the back and front pieces are connected by a welt-like 'box strip'. If yours is of a different type, simply follow the directions, applying them to the contours of your own chair or sofa.

Mark a line with tailor's chalk down the centre of the following: 1) outside back, 2) inside back, 3) seat and 4) front border as in Fig. 6. Repeat on the right side of the fabric.

Outside and inside back. Place the cloth right side out on the outside back of the chair so that the chalk lines match and the seam allowances extend at the top, sides and bottom (Fig. 7) and pin the cloth along the chalk line to the old cover. (The fabric shown has been cut short for a tailored skirt.) Smooth cloth to the sides, keeping the crosswise threads parallel to the floor as you work and pin cloth to upholstery cover along the line of the join on the outside edge of the original upholstery, placing the pins at right angles to the edge (Fig. 8).

Chalk the line of the upholstery join on the right side of the cloth and trim edges to 1.5cm (½in) of the line on irregular shapes (Fig. 9).

Place the section for the inside back in position, pin and mark the top and sides as for the outside back. Leave the tuck-in allowances on the seat for the moment (Fig. 10).

Joining inside and outside back. If there are box strips, place the appropriate strip, right side out, between the inside and outside back. Pin it to the old cover along the centre and then along the edges, following the join line of the old upholstery (Fig. 11). Mark the line with chalk and trim to within 1.5cm (½in).

Pin the strip to the outside and inside back sections along the chalked lines, adjusting if necessary to give a good fit (see Fig. 11). If there is no box strip, pin outside and inside back together.

Outside and inside arms. Pin these, right side out, to the chair (Fig. 12), marking and trimming the edges as on the back.

Pin the box strips together at the top corners (Fig. 13), following the line of the join on the original upholstery. Pin the outside arm to the outside back on one side only (leave A–B free, Fig. 14).

Seat. Place the cloth in position on the seat, right side out, pinning it to the upholstery down the centre and round the edges (see Fig. 14).

Mark the front edge with chalk and trim any excess fabric to within 1.5cm (½in).

Tuck-ins. Pin the tuck-in sections together between the inside back and arms (Fig. 15). (Tuck-in will taper from nothing at the top to the full amount at the bottom.) Then pin the edges of the tuck-ins round the seat to the inside arms and back (Fig. 16).

Front arms. Place these on the chair and pin to the outside arm, the top arm and the inside arm *as far as the beginning of the tuck-in* (Fig. 17).

Front border and skirt. Leave until the other sections have been seamed.

Cushions. See Cushion chapter.

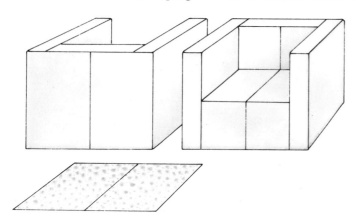

6. Mark chalk lines down centres of main sections.

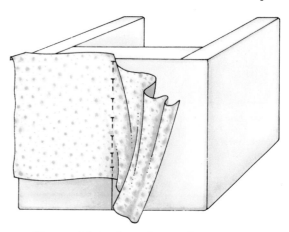

7. Pin outside back section so that chalk marks align on fabric and main cover.

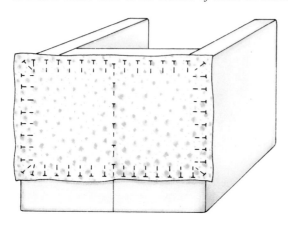

8. Smooth out fabric and fix to main cover with pins at right angles.

9. With irregular shapes, mark line on original join, trim excess.

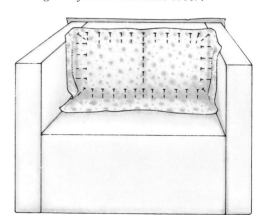

10. Fit inside back section. The tuck-in lies on the seat.

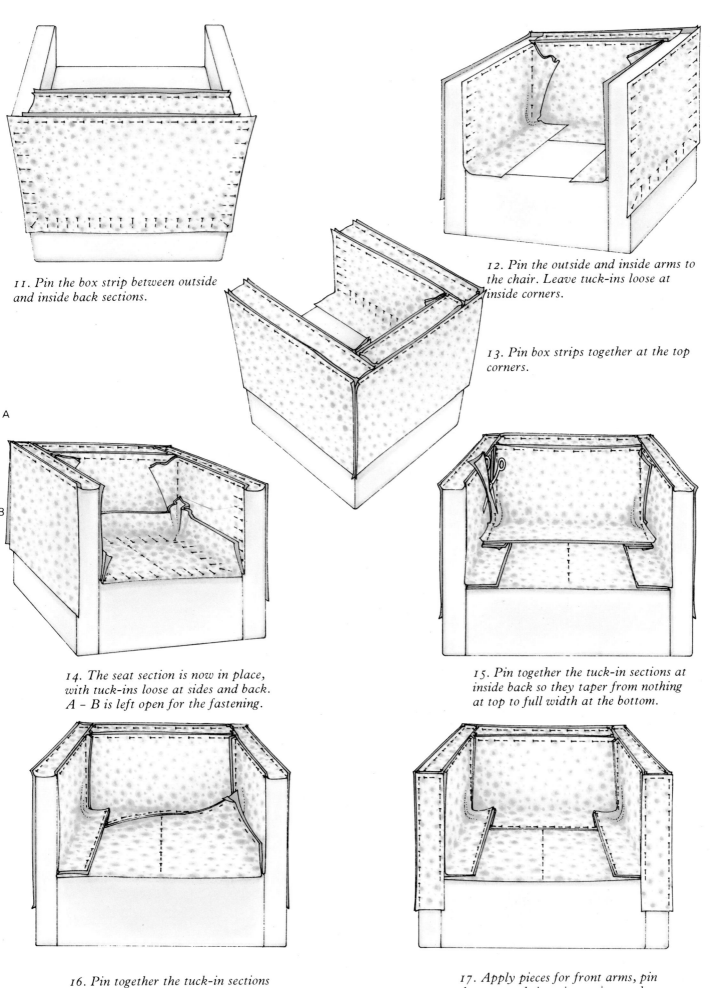

11. Pin the box strip between outside and inside back sections.

12. Pin the outside and inside arms to the chair. Leave tuck-ins loose at inside corners.

13. Pin box strips together at the top corners.

A

B

14. The seat section is now in place, with tuck-ins loose at sides and back. A – B is left open for the fastening.

15. Pin together the tuck-in sections at inside back so they taper from nothing at top to full width at the bottom.

16. Pin together the tuck-in sections around the seat.

17. Apply pieces for front arms, pin down to tuck-in point on inner edge.

117

STITCHING THE COVER

Unpin all sections from the chair and then pin together again off the chair, with right sides facing.

Cut out bias strips and make the piping (see Sewing Guide).

Join the box strips at the front arms and top corners (A to B and B to C, Fig. 18) with right sides together using a plain seam. Press seam turnings open and zigzag or pink edges.

Piping. Apply piping to both long edges of the box strip, clipping the seam turning of the bias casing at the top corners (see Sewing Guide).

Apply other lengths of piping to the side edges of the outside back. At the top corners on the outside back, trim away the piping cord but not its casing by 1.5cm ($\frac{1}{2}$in) to make a flat join.

Main section. Stitch the sections of the cover in the order shown (Fig. 19), placing right sides together and taking 1.5cm ($\frac{1}{2}$in) turnings.

Press the turnings away from the front edges of the chair as you stitch and neaten by zigzag stitch or by straight stitching 5mm ($\frac{1}{4}$in) from the edges, and then trim with pinking shears.

The right-hand edge of the outside back is left for three-quarters of its length for the fastening later on.

The front border. Put the cover on the chair with right side out. Push the tuck-ins into the crevices, leaving the unstitched seam allowances protruding at the front of the chair.

Place the front border section in position and pin to the seat section and its tuck-in (Fig. 20), following the join line of the upholstery.

Pin border to the front arm below the seat tuck-in (Fig. 21a).

Mark and trim the edges to within 1.5cm ($\frac{1}{2}$in) and trim the bottom edge to within 1.5cm ($\frac{1}{2}$in) of the bottom of the chair or 13.5cm ($5\frac{1}{2}$in) of the floor, depending on the finish to be applied. Remove the cover from the chair. Re-pin and stitch border to the cover, inserting piping in the seam (Fig. 21b).

Back opening

Cut a straight strip of fabric twice the length of the opening and 7.5cm (3in) wide.

Stitch strip round the opening, taking 1.5cm ($\frac{1}{2}$in) turnings, Fig. 22a.

Fold under the raw edge of the strip for 1.5cm ($\frac{1}{2}$in), place the fold to the seamline on the wrong side of the cover and machine stitch (Fig. 22b).

Fold the strip so that it lies flat on the outside-arm side and press.

Sew on hooks level with the fold at 5cm (2in) intervals (Fig. 23).

Leave the strip so that it extends on the outside-back side and sew on the eyes level with the inner edge of the binding so that the binding forms an underlap for the opening.

Bottom edge

Apply piping all round the bottom edge, cutting the casing to allow 1.5cm ($\frac{1}{2}$in) extra at each end; turn under the extra amount before making up the piping.

Tailored skirt. If using interfacing, apply to the wrong side of each piece. Following Fig. 24, join the pieces in the following order: 1) insert, 2) outside arm, 3) insert, 4) front, 5) insert, 6) outside arm, 7) insert, 8) outside back. Press turnings away from the inserts.

If lining the skirt, join the lining pieces in the same way and then, with right sides together, stitch to the skirt along both short edges and the bottom, taking 1.5cm ($\frac{1}{2}$in) turnings. Turn right side out.

If not lining the skirt, turn up hem and stitch.

Fold the inserts to form an inverted

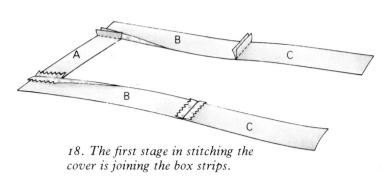

18. The first stage in stitching the cover is joining the box strips.

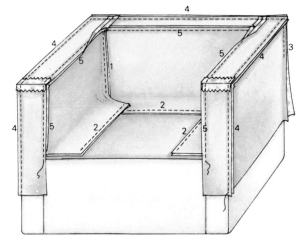

19. Stitch sections together in order shown, enclose piping on exposed seams.

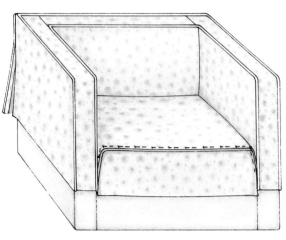

20. The partly made cover is put on the chair for fitting the front border to the seat.

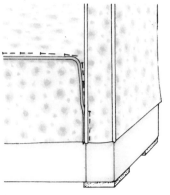

21a. Joining front arm and tuck-in.

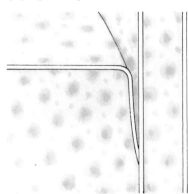

21b. Piped front border.

pleat as shown (Fig. 25). Press.
Stitch the skirt to the cover, taking 1.5cm (½in) turnings, matching the inverted pleats to the corners. At the opening, sew on a hook and eye and fasten the insert in position (Fig. 26).

Plain finished bottom. Trim the short ends of the strips at an angle so that they will clear the chair legs when tied underneath (Fig. 27a).

Make a narrow hem on each short end and then a wider hem on the inner long edges to form casing for tape (Fig. 27b). Stitch the remaining long edges to the appropriate edge of the cover, right sides facing (Fig. 28).

Insert a length of tape, sufficient to go round bottom of chair, through the hems of the inner edges of the strips. Put the cover on the chair and tie tape in one corner (Fig. 29).

Flounce. Make up and attach flounce as described on page 148 in the Sewing Guide. Leave edges open below fastening.

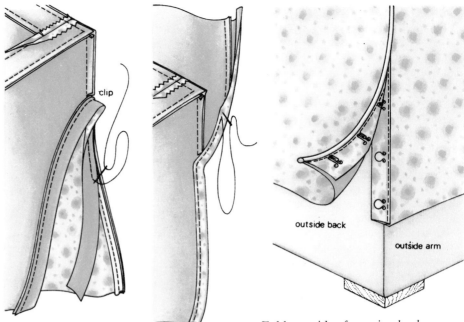

22. Clip seam turning above opening so edges of opening can be finished by binding with a long strip.

23. Fold one side of opening back, leaving other side as underlap. Apply hooks and eyes.

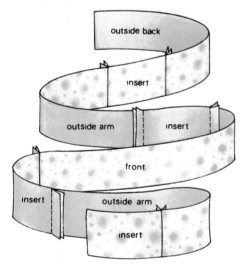

24. For tailored skirt, join the sections together, as shown.

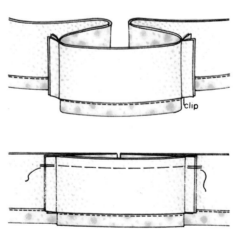

25. Fold inserts to form an inverted pleat, as shown. Clip turnings above hem.

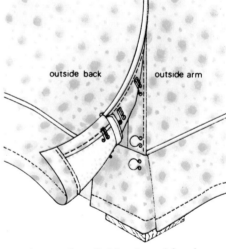

26. At opening, finish edge with a hem and apply hooks and eye.

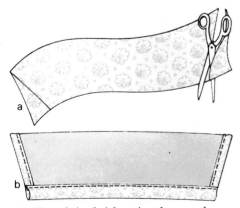

27. For plain finish, trim short ends at an angle and hem them. Make a wider hem at bottom for casing.

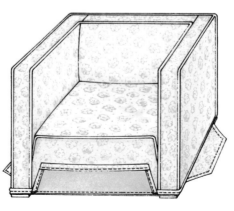

28. Stitch strips to appropriate edges of cover to fit between chair legs.

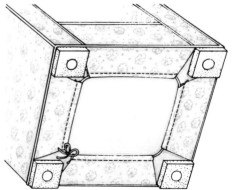

29. Insert tape through casings, and tie at corner.

119

SCROLL-ARMCHAIRS

The method for making this type of cover is very similar to box-armed chairs with the omission of box strips. If, when pinning the inside back to the outside back, you find fullness at the corners, neaten it into small pleats (Fig. 1).

At the arm, cut into the inside-back fabric at the sides so that it can be wrapped round the edge of the chair smoothly. Carefully cut the curve over the top of the arm and then down to the seat so there is the normal seam allowance at the top but the full tuck-in allowance at the bottom (Fig. 2).

Repeat on the inside arm (Fig. 3). Then pin inside back fabric to inside arm. Clip the seam allowance over the crown of the arm (Fig. 3).

Piping. When making up the cover, apply the piping all round the outside back and front arms, between the outside and inside arms and all round the front border.

Finish the cover in the way described for a box-armed chair.

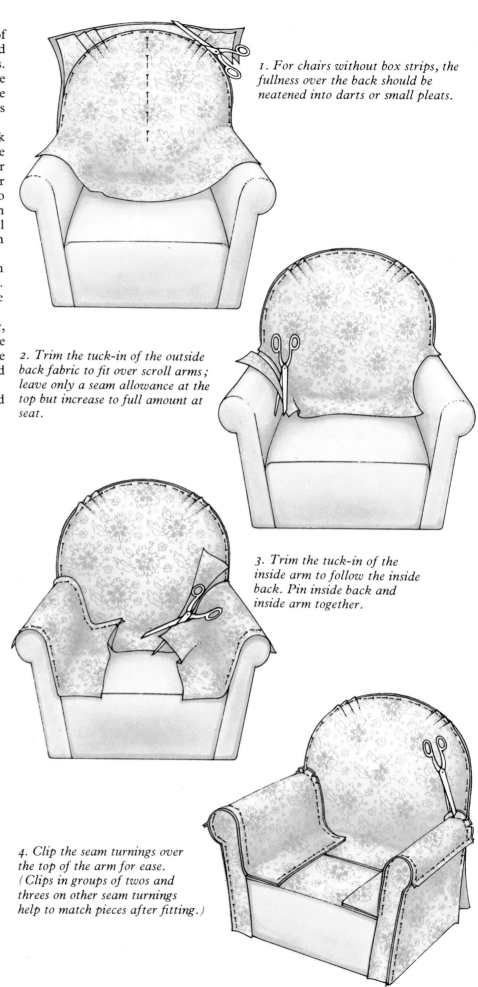

1. For chairs without box strips, the fullness over the back should be neatened into darts or small pleats.

2. Trim the tuck-in of the outside back fabric to fit over scroll arms; leave only a seam allowance at the top but increase to full amount at seat.

3. Trim the tuck-in of the inside arm to follow the inside back. Pin inside back and inside arm together.

4. Clip the seam turnings over the top of the arm for ease. (Clips in groups of twos and threes on other seam turnings help to match pieces after fitting.)

Several types of chair and sofa styles are shown here. Loose covers may be made for such styles by following the join lines on the main cover and following the method described in this chapter.

Upholstery

Upholstery combines the techniques of soft furnishing and carpentry and is a craft which takes many years to learn. However, there are several basic jobs which can be done by the novice, including repairs, re-covering simple pieces of furniture, and even some complete re-upholstery on small things such as stools and dining chairs.

Upholstery falls into two distinct categories, according to the type of padding used. The traditional padding is horsehair, involving complicated techniques to shape it and hold it in place to give several years' wear.

The modern padding material is foam rubber which is quick to apply but also quick to wear out – its life expectancy is three to five years in comparison with 15–20 years or more with horsehair stuffing.

You can substitute foam padding for horsehair as it is so much easier to apply, but this should not be done to anything of antique value on which you should retain the original method of upholstery.

MATERIALS

The choice of cover fabric for upholstery is more limited than in any other area of soft furnishing because the fabric has to be firmly woven and hardwearing. Suitable fabrics include velvet, brocade, damask, linen, heavy cotton, twill and wool; and these should be specifically recommended for upholstery by the manufacturer. On simple pieces of furniture such as drop-in seats you can also use needlepoint and leather.

Other materials likely to be needed are webbing, hessian (burlap), calico (muslin in America), wadding and bottoming. These are described below and most of them have to be bought from a specialist upholstery stockist.

Webbing (Fig. 1) is the foundation of all upholstery applied to an open frame. It spans the frame in interwoven strands and if one strand is broken or loose the upholstery sags. In traditional upholstery the webbing is woven from jute or flax; its modern counterpart is made from rubber which is stretchy and gives additional resilience when used with foam rubber.

Web strainer. To apply woven webbing so that it is really taut, a special strainer or a small block of wood must be used (Fig. 2).

Hessian (burlap) is used to cover the frame over woven webbing as a platform for the stuffing. It is usually not used with foam rubber. Use real upholstery hessian (burlap) which is

available in different weights. Use 250g (10oz) to 90cm sq (1sq yd).

Horsehair is the traditional padding material but these days it is expensive and not easy to obtain so it is often recycled or mixed with other animal hair. You can usually re-use old horsehair, washing it and sanitizing it in nappy powder if you wish.

Foam rubber is the padding used mostly in modern furniture. Buy seating-grade upholstery foam.

Calico (muslin in USA) is placed over the padding to shape it and make a smooth surface for the top and main cover.

Wadding is a fluffy material with a skin-like backing which forms additional padding between the calico and main cover. It also helps to prevent stray horsehairs from working through and making the surface prickly.

Bottoming is black fabric, usually linen, attached underneath seats to finish off.

Tintacks (never nails) are used to attach most upholstery materials to the wooden frame. Small-headed tacks – 'fine' – with shanks of 1cm ($\frac{3}{8}$in) are for covering fabrics and large-headed ones – 'improved' – of 1.5cm ($\frac{1}{2}$in) are for webbing, to give greater strength. If possible, use tacks described as 'cut' because these have shaped points (Fig. 3) to make them easy to press into the wood with your fingers before hammering.

The hammer need not be a special upholstery one but it should have a small head to avoid hitting the wood around the tack head when you hammer it flat.

Chisel. A ripping chisel or an old blunt wood chisel (or screwdriver with a mallet) is used to remove old tacks.

Spring needle. If replacing webbing on a seat with springs, a curved needle (Fig. 4) is needed to re-sew the springs to the webbing.

It is possible to use a heavy straight needle (providing the twine will pass through its eye) but each stitch will have to be made in two stages, passing it down through the webbing, withdrawing it completely before passing it under the spring coil, and pushing it up again. With a curved needle all this can be done in one stage. A curved needle is also needed when applying horsehair padding.

Button needle. To replace buttons, use a long needle of about 15–20cm (6–8in) with a point at each end (Fig. 5) which enables it to be pushed back, eye-end first, through the upholstery without having to pull it completely out and turn it round in order to re-insert it.

Unfortunately, because of the thickness of the upholstery, there is no substitute.

Twine is used with the needles. Use proper upholsterer's waxed twine in the weight recommended for the job by the manufacturer.

TECHNICAL HINTS

Temporary tacking is a term used to describe the process of partially hammering the tack down in the required position when first placing materials on the frame. It is then easy to remove if you wish to adjust the fabric later.

To remove old nails hold the chisel parallel to the length of wood and as flat as possible, and place the tip under a tack head.

Tap the end of the handle smartly with the mallet (Fig. 6), tilting the tip upwards gradually as you do so. This should lift the tack sufficiently for you to prize it out with pincers or a tack lifter.

It is important to remove all the tacks to make room for the new ones. Do not be tempted to re-use old tacks – they will probably be bent and may also be rusty.

When stripping old upholstery, cover the floor with newspaper and put old useless stuffing and tacks immediately into a box for disposal.

Never kneel on the floor without first checking for stray tacks.

Have the furniture at a convenient working height, ensuring that it cannot slip when you hammer.

To prevent accidents, put corks onto the points of needles and never leave needles sticking out from your work. Make any repairs to the frame before starting the new upholstery.

ESTIMATING MATERIALS

Main or top cover. To calculate the quantity of fabric, measure either the total area to be covered or the old cover and add 10cm (4in) each way for turnings.

Calico (muslin in USA). Fabric allowance is the same as for main cover.

Webbing. See replacing webbing, pages 124–125.

Hessian (burlap). Allow a rectangle to the measurements of the frame plus 3cm (1in) each way.

Foam rubber. Have it cut to the size of your template (see page 132).

Wadding. Same size as seat area.

Bottoming. Allow a rectangle to the frame size plus 2cm (¾in) each way.

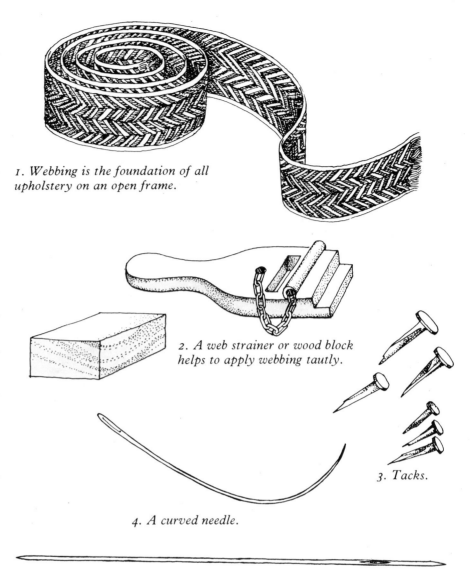

1. Webbing is the foundation of all upholstery on an open frame.

2. A web strainer or wood block helps to apply webbing tautly.

3. Tacks.

4. A curved needle.

5. A double-pointed needle.

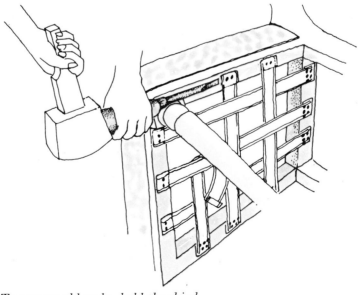

6. To remove old tacks, hold the chisel parallel to wood to avoid gouging it, and tip of blade under tack head. Hammer handle with mallet to loosen tack.

REPLACING WOVEN WEBBING

This is simple to do on an empty frame with the upholstery taken off. However, it is not worth removing good upholstery just to replace a little webbing; this can be done without disturbing the upholstery if the webbing is attached to the underside (Fig. 1a) of the frame but it is more difficult if tacked to the upper side (Fig. 1b).

For every strand to be replaced, measure across the frame in the exact position of each previous or existing one and add 5cm (2in) for turnings; add a further 15cm (6in) to the total amount for fitting on the web strainer. You will also need ten 1.5cm (½in) improved head tacks per strand, as well as a curved needle and some twine if the seat has springs.

To attach webbing to the underside, first remove the existing strands. If they are sewn to springs, cut through all the stitches holding them.

Do not cut out individual strips if attaching more than one; leave the webbing as a continuous length.

Turn under the end 2.5cm (1in) and place in position of the strip on the frame so that the folded end is about halfway across the rail, as in Fig. 2. Trying to avoid the original tack holes, attach to the frame with three tacks through the fold; add two more to form the pattern shown.

Push any springs to one side and lay the webbing flat across the frame, interweaving it with any strands already on the frame. Then either wrap it round a wood block as in Fig. 2, or insert it into the strainer.

Hold the strainer with the handle away from you, make a loop in the webbing, put it through the slot and insert the peg (Fig. 3a). Turn the strainer handle towards you, adjust the length of the webbing by pulling round the peg; the webbing should be taut across the frame with the edge of the strainer against it (Fig. 3b). (Adjust the tension to match existing strands.) Turn the wood block or the strainer handle down and insert three tacks through a single thickness of webbing into the frame in a line halfway across the rail. Hammer the tacks flat.

Cut off the webbing 2.5cm (1in) from the tacks, fold down the turning and insert two more tacks through the double thickness and above the other three.

Push any springs under the webbing and insert the other strands of webbing in the same way (Fig. 4).

Sew the springs to the webbing by

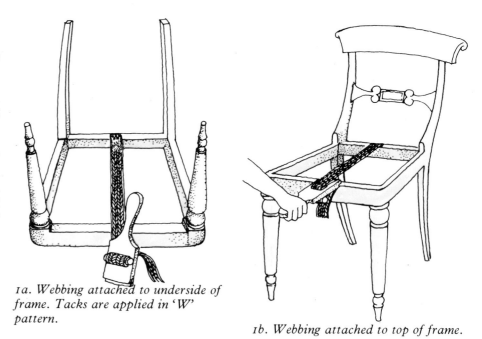

1a. *Webbing attached to underside of frame. Tacks are applied in 'W' pattern.*

1b. *Webbing attached to top of frame.*

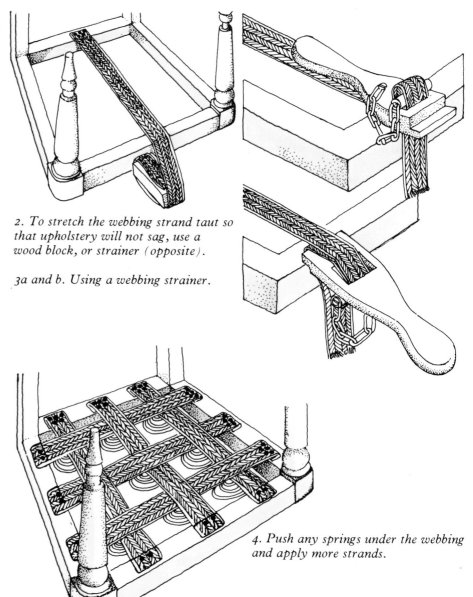

2. *To stretch the webbing strand taut so that upholstery will not sag, use a wood block, or strainer (opposite).*

3a and b. *Using a webbing strainer.*

4. *Push any springs under the webbing and apply more strands.*

inserting the needle under the nearest coil, bringing it out and making two more stitches round the spring as shown (Fig. 5). Tie the ends in a slip knot (Fig. 6).

Attach all springs in this way.

Webbing attached to the upper side of the frame cannot be replaced in the same position without removing the entire upholstery. However, you can make a satisfactory repair by attaching it to the inside face of the frame (Fig. 7). Interlace the webbing tape, if possible.

Attach the tacks in the required position, as close to the upper edge of the seat as possible without splitting the wood.

REPLACING RUBBER WEBBING

Rubber webbing may be applied with special clips which slot into grooves in the frame, or with tacks if there are no existing grooves.

Measure the distance to be spanned by each strip of webbing from the centre of one rail to the centre of the opposite one.

Subtract one-tenth of the measurement to allow for tensioning and then add 3cm (1in) for attaching.

Clips. You will need a clip for each end of the strand. Insert the ends into the clips and close in a vice (Fig. 1a) or with pincers.

Place one clip into the groove, stretch the strand across the frame to the opposite groove and push in the clip (Fig. 1b).

Tacks. You will need eight 1.5cm (½in) improved-head tacks for each strand.

Method

Draw a line across the strip 1.5cm (½in) from one end, then measure from this line to the required length of the strip and draw a line.

Subtract approximately 2cm (½in) for tensioning and make another mark across the strip.

Place the end in position on the frame so that the first line is halfway across the rail (Fig. 2a).

Apply four tacks through the line, being careful to hammer the heads absolutely flat to avoid their cutting the rubber.

Lay the strand across the frame and stretch so that the second mark is in the centre of the rail; apply with four tacks along the line (Fig. 2b). Cut off the excess webbing 1.5cm (½in) from the tacks.

Interlace subsequent strips.

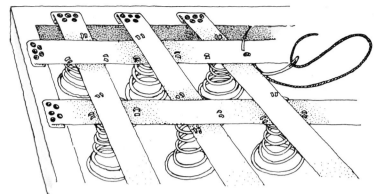

5. Sew springs to webbing.

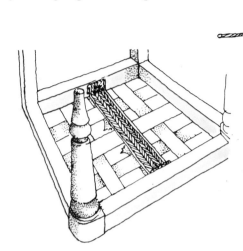

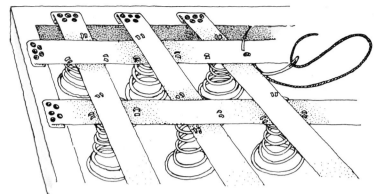

6. Tie ends in a slip knot.

7. To repair webbing attached to upper side of frame without disturbing upholstery, attach it underneath, tacking to side face of frame.

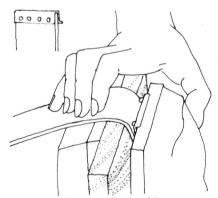

1a. Attach clip to end of rubber webbing with a vice.

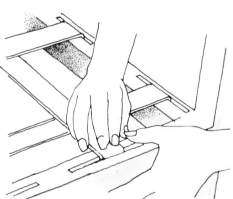

1b. Insert ends of rubber webbing into groove in frame.

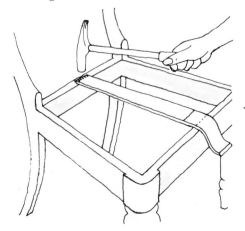

2a. If the furniture has no grooves, position rubber webbing on frame.

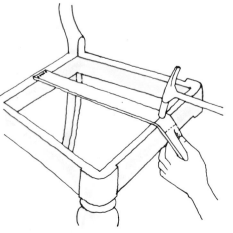

2b. Tack webbing on one edge, then stretch to give tension.

REPLACING BUTTONS

You will need a button needle (double-pointed straight upholsterer's needle), 15–20cm (6–8in) long; upholsterer's twine 30cm (12in) long, plus a button mould of suitable size if the original button is lost.

Method

To cover the button mould, look for a piece of cover fabric underneath the piece of furniture you are working on or, if there is an outside back panel, it might be worth undoing some of the slipstitching holding it on. (You will probably find some spare fabric on the turnings underneath.)

Cover the mould, following manufacturer's instructions.

Thread the needle with twine. Insert the unthreaded point end into the upholstery at the button position and pass through the padding until the end emerges at the other side (Fig. 1a).

Holding the second end of twine, pull the needle through until you can see the eye (Fig. 1b); do not pull out completely but push back through the padding at an angle to come out 5mm ($\frac{1}{4}$in) from the original entry (Fig. 1c). (The twine will thus have made a loop round the padding inside.)

Pull out the needle and adjust the twine so that both ends are equal. Thread one end through the shank of the button and tie to the other end in a slip knot (Fig. 2). Pull the knot tight until the button is in the required position. Tie the twine in an ordinary knot to secure it, cut the ends short and tuck under the button.

N.B. If the back covering panel has already been removed, start as described above but pull the needle right out on the back and then re-insert it 5mm ($\frac{1}{4}$in) away to emerge 5mm ($\frac{1}{4}$in) from the original entry; insert a small roll of waste fabric, about 3cm (1in) wide, under the stitch made on the back to prevent it from pulling through.

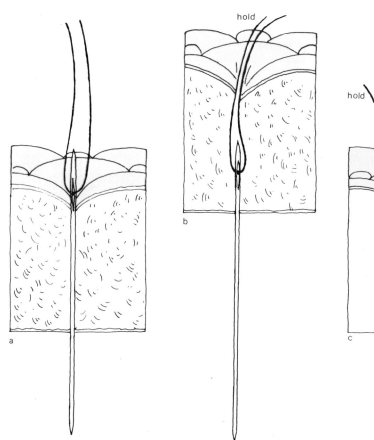

1a. Insert needle at button position.
1b. Holding twine end, pass needle through to other side as far as the eye.
1c. Push needle back to come out 5mm ($\frac{1}{4}$in) from entry point.

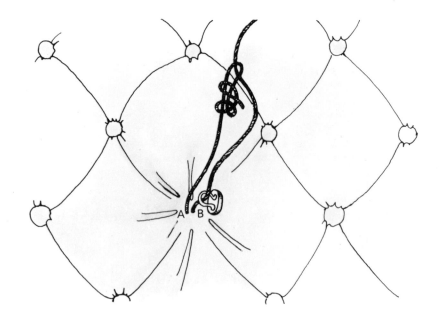

2. Thread one end of twine through button shank and tie with other end in a slip knot. Pull knot tight.

RE-COVERING A DROP-IN SEAT

You will need a piece of fabric the overall size of the seat plus 15cm (6in) each way; about 25g (1oz) of 1cm ($\frac{3}{8}$in) fine-headed tacks; bottoming and wadding 2cm ($\frac{3}{4}$in) larger each way than seat; G-clamps, tack lifter, tack hammer.

Method

Preparation. Remove tintacks holding bottoming and top cover, as described on page 123.

If there is a thin layer of wadding over a calico (muslin USA) under cover, remove this too. If the wadding is thick, with no calico below it, leave it on the seat.

Mark the centre of each edge of the right side of new cover, and bottoming. Mark the centre of each edge of the seat frame on underside, then draw lines on the underside round the perimeter 2.5cm (1in) from the outer edge as a guide for placing the tacks.

Attaching cover. Lay out the fabric flat, wrong side facing up, and place first the wadding (fluffy side down) on top of the fabric, and then the seat frame, also upside down. Align the centre marks.

Turn up the fabric along the back edge and attach to the frame with temporary tacks 2.5cm (1in) apart along the marked line, working outwards from the centre to within 5cm (2in) of the corners (Fig. 1).

Lift the frame so that it rests on the back edge and smooth the fabric over the seat to the front edge (Fig. 2).

Keeping the frame in the same position and pulling the fabric taut, attach to the underside of the frame in the same way as the back edge. Repeat for each side edge, keeping the fabric straight and taut.

At each corner, pull the fabric down hard diagonally and tack the corner to the underside. Fold the excess fabric on each side of the point into a pleat, trimming some from inside as shown (Fig. 3a).

Tack down (Fig. 3b). If the fabric near corners now wrinkles, lift out the tacks nearest the wrinkles, smooth the fabric down and re-tack.

Run the palm of your hand across the seat to check that the fabric is smooth and taut – if it wrinkles, lift the tacks and tighten it. When you are satisfied, hammer all the tacks flat.

Trim the excess fabric to 1cm ($\frac{3}{8}$in) of the tacks.

The bottoming. Fold under each edge of the bottoming for 1cm ($\frac{3}{8}$in). Centre it with right side up on the underside of the frame and attach it, placing the tacks close to the folds and 5cm (2in) apart, with one in each corner (Fig. 4).

The seat is now complete.

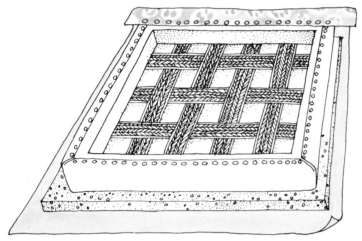

1. Lay out fabric, wrong side up. Centre wadding, fluffy side down. Lay seat face down on top. Turn up back edge of fabric and tack to frame.

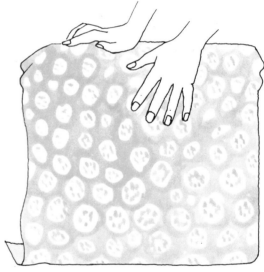

2. Turn frame on back edge. Smooth fabric over the seat to front edge. Attach to underside of frame.

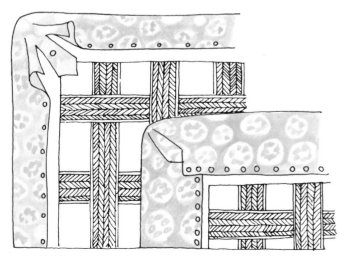

3a and b. Pull fabric hard diagonally over corner of frame; tack. Fold down excess on each side into pleats, trimming fabric inside. Tack down.

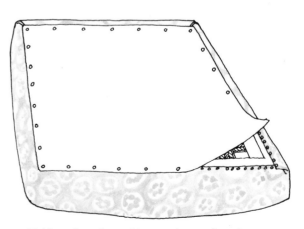

4. Fold under edges of bottoming and tack to underside of frame to cover raw edges of top fabric.

RE-COVERING AN UPHOLSTERED SEAT

You will need cover fabric (measure total area, add 10cm (4in) each way); wadding to overall size of seat, bottoming 2cm ($\frac{3}{4}$in) larger each way than seat; about 25g (1oz) of 1cm ($\frac{3}{8}$in) fine-headed tacks; tack lifter, tack hammer. Braid (if required) to fit perimeter of seat plus 5cm (2in); fabric glue.

Method

Preparation. Turn the chair upside down and remove tintacks holding bottoming (see page 123). If the old cover was also attached to the underside of the frame, remove all its tacks too. If it was attached to the side fabric of the frame, pull off the braid covering the tacks, turn the chair on its side and remove the tacks from the side now uppermost. Repeat on each side, turning the chair so that the side you are working on is uppermost. Remove the wadding under the old cover and discard.

The new cover. Place the chair right way up. Tease the edges of the wadding with your fingers to soften them and place it on the seat with the fluffy side facing up. Centre the new cover, right side up, over the seat. Temporary-tack cover to the side face or underneath the frame, as appropriate, in centre of each edge (Fig. 1). Temporary-tack the back edge, placing the tacks in a straight line just above the show-wood (the wood that shows), if attaching to the side face. Tack 1.5cm ($\frac{1}{2}$in) from the outside edge if attaching underneath. In either case, stop 5cm (2in) from the back uprights. Smooth the fabric across the seat to the front edge and pull down hard, adjusting the tack at the centre if necessary.
Temporary-tack the cloth to the frame to within 5cm (2in) of each corner. Repeat for each side edge, keeping the fabric smooth and straight.

The back corners. To cut the fabric to fit it round the back uprights, turn up the corner diagonally so that the fold touches the inner edge of the upright (Fig. 2).
Cut from the point to the fold. Take resulting triangles to each side of the upright and pull down firmly. Fold them under to form a neat line with the upright and press the folds with your fingers (Fig. 3).
Lift up the fabric again and cut away the excess to within 1cm ($\frac{3}{8}$in) of the fold. Refold and temporary-tack (Fig.

4). Add more temporary tacks to meet those already placed, adjusting any if the fabric needs smoothing down to eliminate wrinkles.

Front corners. You will also have surplus fabric at the front corners. If these are square, fold the fabric in a single pleat (Fig. 5).
If they are rounded, fold the fabric in an inverted pleat (Fig. 6). Tack down. When you are satisfied with the fit of the cover and have eliminated all wrinkles, add a tack to each space so the tacks are now 1.5cm ($\frac{1}{2}$in) apart. Hammer all tacks flat.
Using a handyman's knife or razor blade, trim away the surplus fabric close to the edge of the tacks (Fig. 7).

Braid. If the chair is to be finished with braid, fold under one end of the braid for 1cm ($\frac{3}{8}$in). Place it on the chair at a corner so that it covers the tacks and raw edge of the fabric. Insert a tack inside the fold (Fig. 8). Spread fabric glue on the wrong side of the braid for about 15cm (6in). Hold the braid taut at the end of the sticky section and press down in position on the chair (Fig. 9). Repeat all round the edge. Turn under the end and stick down, holding it in place with a temporary tack until the adhesive dries. Remove the tack.

Bottoming. Turn the chair upside down. Centre the bottoming on the underside of the frame and temporary-tack through the single thickness at the centre of each edge.
Starting on the back edge, turn under the raw edge so that the fold is 1cm ($\frac{3}{8}$in) from the outside edge.
Temporary-tack to within 2.5cm (1in) of the legs, placing the tacks 5cm (2in) apart. Repeat along the front, clipping the turnings where the frame curves, and then on the sides.
To fit the fabric at the legs, turn it back diagonally in a fold touching the inner edge of the legs. Cut from the point to the fold (Fig. 10), fold under points on each side of the leg and tack.

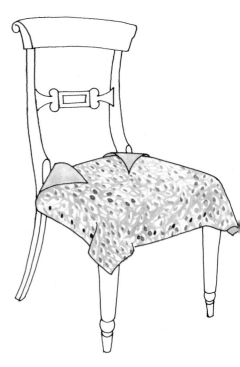

1. Tack new cover to centre of frame, on side face or underneath.

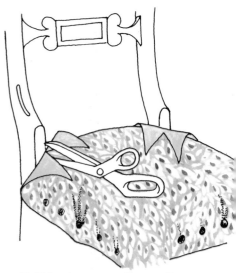

2. Fold back corners diagonally at uprights and cut from point to fold.

3. Fold under the triangles of fabric to make neat folds.

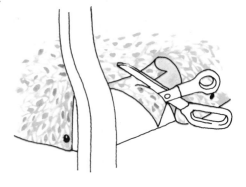

4. Trim away the excess fabric to within 1cm ($\frac{3}{8}$in) of folds. Tack down.

128

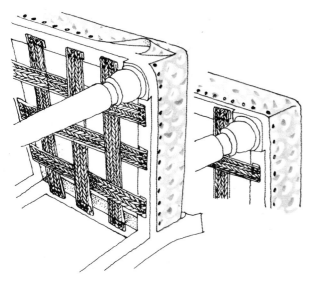

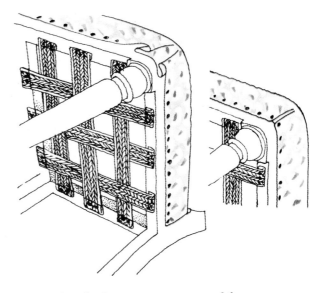

5. *Pleating the front corners on square frame.*

6. *Pleating the front corners on round frame.*

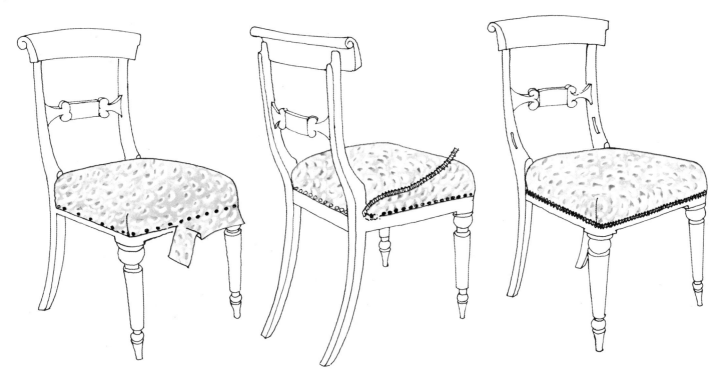

7. *Trim away excess fabric below tacks.*

8. *Insert tack inside folded end of braid and stick braid down.*

9. *Braid is applied to hide tacks and raw edges of fabric.*

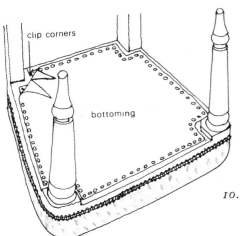

clip corners

bottoming

10. *Neatening bottom of chair.*

RE-UPHOLSTERING A DROP-IN SEAT

You will need all the materials and tools listed on page 127, plus webbing, webbing stretcher, improved tacks, a rectangle of hessian (burlap) the overall seat size plus 1.5cm (½in) all round, twine, curved needle, horsehair, calico (muslin) and G-clamps.

Method

Remove the seat from the frame and secure upside down on a work surface with G-clamps.

Remove all tacks holding the old materials (see Fig. 6, page 123), and turn the seat the other way up to remove hessian (burlap) and webbing. Mark both sides of the seat with a line 2.5cm (1in) from the outer edge and mark the centre of each rail (Fig. 1).

Webbing. Replace the webbing as described previously.

Hessian (burlap). Centre the hessian (burlap) on the seat above the webbing and attach with a temporary tack in the middle of each edge (Fig. 2).

Turn up the back edge so that the fold lies along the marked line and insert a tack through the fold at the centre.

Stretch the fold to the corners of the marked line and tack through the double thickness. Insert more tacks at 2.5cm (1in) intervals (Fig. 3).

Pull the hessian (burlap) to the front of the seat, keeping the grain straight, and tack it at the centre of the marked line through single thickness only (Fig. 4). Stretch to the front corners and tack and insert more tacks at 4cm (1½in) intervals.

Fold the turning over the tacks and add more between those already there.

Turn up one side so that the fold lies along the marked line. Tack down at 2.5cm (1in) intervals. Stretch to the opposite edge of the frame and apply as the front edge.

Padding. To make loops to hold the stuffing in place, thread the needle with enough twine to fit the perimeter of the seat plus half as much again.

Starting at the point shown (Fig. 5), make a stitch and then tie the end of the twine to the main length in a slip knot. Tighten the slip knot and work round the edge of the seat, making backstitches (see Sewing Guide) in the places shown, and leaving loops between them large enough to insert two fingers. Finish off with another slip knot.

Tease out handfuls of horsehair to ensure there are no lumps and insert under loops (Fig. 6) until packed to the edges of the seat (Fig. 7). Insert more horsehair in the middle of the seat to make a dome shape about 5cm (2in) high.

Calico (American muslin). Place this over the horsehair and secure with a temporary tack in the centre of each side face of the frame (Fig. 8).

Turn the frame upside down and tack the back edge, placing the tacks 2.5cm (2in) short of the corners (Fig. 9).

Turn the seat to rest on the back edge, release the temporary tack on the front edge and smooth the calico with the palm of the hand over the stuffing and underneath the seat. Temporary-tack just outside the marked line at the centre (Fig. 10), stretch to 5cm (2in) of the corner, pull down and tack.

Add more tacks at 2.5cm (1in) intervals and repeat the procedure on the sides, being careful to keep the grain straight. There should be no looseness now when the palm of the hand is run across the seat, and the stuffing will have flattened.

To complete the corners, pull the calico (American muslin) diagonally over the edge of the frame and then pull the excess round to the side edges. Tack 1.5cm (½in) from the corners, fold the excess into a single pleat and cut off the inside of the pleat in a triangular piece between the fold and the tack (Fig. 11a).

Tack down the pleat (Fig. 11b). Hammer all temporary tacks down.

Wadding and top cover. Attach these as described on page 128, finishing off with bottoming.

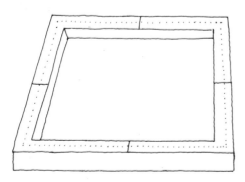

1. Mark guidelines on frame.

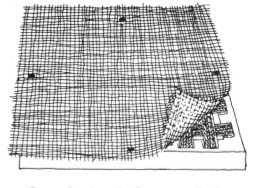

2. Centre hessian (burlap) over the frame and tack.

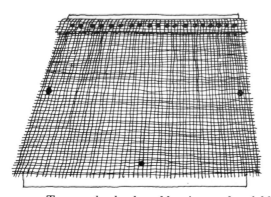

3. Turn up back edge of hessian so that fold lies along marked line.

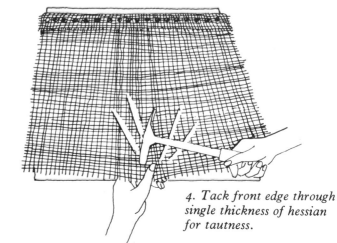

4. Tack front edge through single thickness of hessian for tautness.

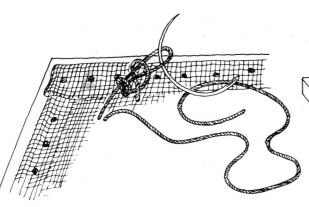

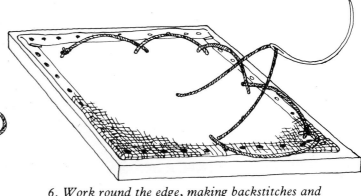

5. To start loops for stuffing, make a stitch in hessian and tie slip knot.

6. Work round the edge, making backstitches and leaving loops between them.

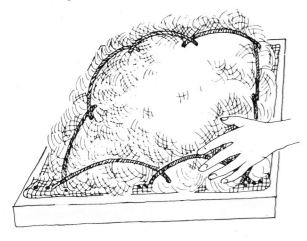

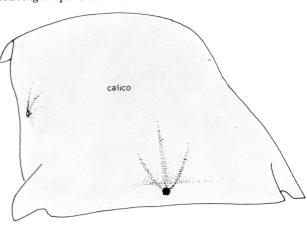

7. Tease out handfuls of stuffing and insert under loops.

8. Apply calico over stuffing and temporary tack to frame.

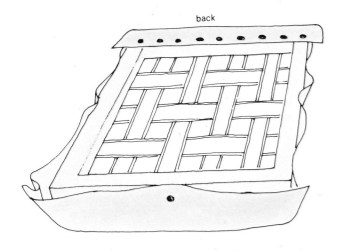

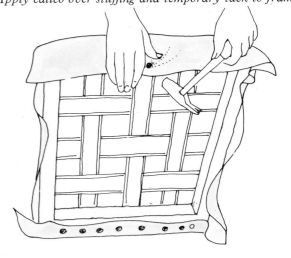

9. Turn frame upside down and tack back edge just outside marked line.

10. Rest the frame on back edge, smooth calico over seat to front and tack at centre.

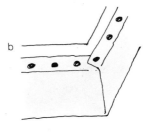

11a and b. Complete the corners by folding into a pleat and then trimming away the excess inside the pleat to reduce bulk.

RE-UPHOLSTERING OVERSTUFFED SEAT WITH FOAM

'Overstuffed' means that the padding is built up on top of the seat frame, as shown in Fig. 1.

You will need: the materials and equipment on pages 122-3, plus a template of the seat (see below), 5cm (2in) thick seating-grade foam cut from template, extra calico (muslin) and tacks, rubber webbing, fabric glue.

Method

Preparation. Remove all the tacks holding the old upholstery. If the seat frame has small high sections at the front corners, these will have to be cut off level with the rest of the frame (Fig. 2) (N.B. the method is obviously not advisable for fine furniture.)

To make a template of the seat, lay a piece of paper over it and draw round the edge of the frame. Draw another line 1.5cm (½in) outside this one, excluding the uprights. Use this second line as the outline for the foam (Fig. 3).

Webbing. Replace the old webbing with rubber webbing, tacking it to the top side of the seat (page 125).

Calico (muslin). Cut a 10cm (4in) wide strip of calico (muslin) to fit each edge of the foam allowing 2.5cm (1in) extra at the front corners (Fig. 4).

Applying the foam. Mark a 5cm (2in) border round the top of the foam on the side which will be uppermost when it is on the seat, and cover the border with glue.

Fold the calico strips in half lengthwise and stick them on the foam so that the fold lines are on the edge and the rest overlaps, with 2.5cm (1in) extending at the front corners (Fig. 5).

Place the foam on the seat, pushing it tightly against the back uprights.

Roll the side edges of the foam under the front and pull the calico down firmly so that it is flat on the frame to give a firm round edge to the foam. Temporary-tack it to the frame at the centre, 1.5cm from the top of the wood (Fig. 6).

Repeat on the back and on each side of the seat. Return to the front and apply more tacks at 2.5cm (1in) intervals to within 5cm (2in) of the corners. Don't worry if the foam rises from the seat at this stage – it will flatten when the calico (American muslin) lining is applied.

Repeat on the back and sides. Pull the fabric round at the front corners, cut off the excess and tack (Fig. 7).

Calico lining, wadding, top cover: apply as described earlier.

1. *Overstuffing means built-up padding.*

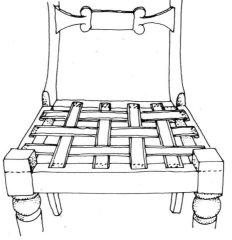

2. *If frame has high sections at front corners, trim them off.*

3. *Cut a paper template 1.5cm (½in) larger than the seat area.*

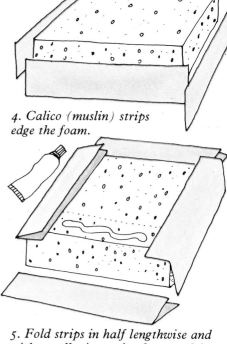

4. *Calico (muslin) strips edge the foam.*

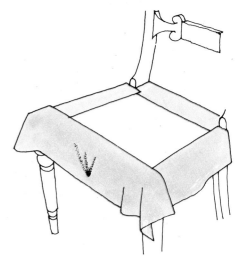

5. *Fold strips in half lengthwise and stick to adhesive on border round foam.*

6. *Roll foam under and pull strips down firmly. Tack to frame.*

7. *Pull strips round front corners. Cut off excess and tack.*

Small areas of upholstery can sometimes be undertaken without much difficulty. This sewing chair is a good example: not only is the area involved not very large, but there are no complicated contours.
Note that instead of a braid trim, the raw edges are disguised with thin strips of bamboo.

The wicker armchair is a delightfully simple yet effective upholstery creation. The 'upholstery' is made by sandwiching wadding between cover and lining which are cut out following the contours of the chair in much the same way as loose covers (described earlier) are cut out. The lining is made in the cover fabric since it can be seen through the wicker. Buttoning holds the padding, cover and lining together and adds to the visual interest.

Quilted fabric adds softness to upholstery and does not require any additional techniques. The wrapped knob foot is an unusual finishing touch.

Sewing guide

This chapter is designed to be a useful guide for all levels of sewing ability and experience. The basic techniques are explained – beginning with how to sew a flat seam – as well as the methods of making more complicated seams, hemming and attaching various edgings.

The chapter's contents are listed below. While particularly relevant to soft furnishings, the guide is also a general reference for all types of home sewing.

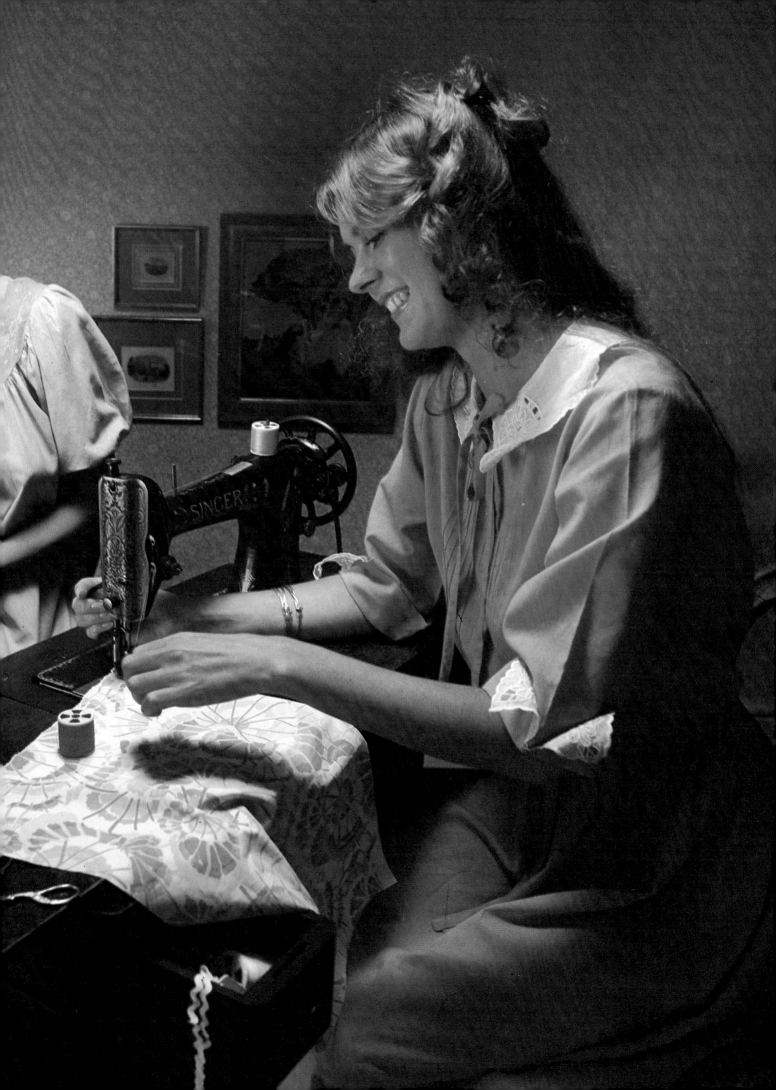

Studying the mixture of fabrics in this room is a valuable lesson in the use of colours. Brown and grey are the pervading hues but bright orange and red are dominant : even the flowers echo the vivid spots of colour. The effect of this daring combination is decidedly warm and welcoming.

The bedspreads and cushions shown above are made using techniques described earlier in this book. They also show how clever design and choice of colouring contribute to the successful decoration of a room. Conventional beds have been replaced by mattresses set on carpeted platforms. The fitted bedspreads and wealth of cushions make the beds into studio couches during the daytime.

Right : this window recess is a favourite seat for Tricia Guild's daughter, Lisa. The flat, buttoned cushion and Roman blind have the same pattern as the walls, but the blind has a splendidly decorative border made with appliqué and zigzag stitching and this gives the area its brightness. (Roman blind making is described on page 72).

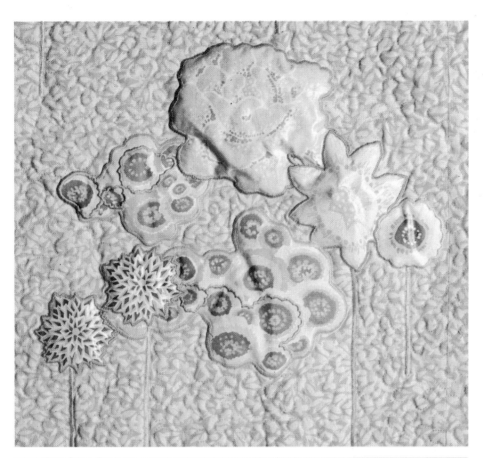

Appliqué is a popular decorative device at Designers Guild. Here, 'flowers' are created using printed fabrics. The raw edges are concealed with decorative stitching which also makes the flower 'stems'.

Fabric applied to walls in the manner shown on the left has the advantage of being removable for laundering. The fabric is made into conventional cased headed curtains, (described on page 88), but casing rods are attached at both ends instead of only one. The fabric is unlined and each width has a small hem along the selvedge. Several widths can be gathered on the same rod.

Seams

A simple flat seam is the most commonly used seam in home sewing. It is unobtrusive, with no lines of stitching showing on the right side. It is the best seam to use for joining widths of fabric when making curtains or loose covers.

It is made by placing the fabric with right sides together and stitching through both layers of fabric. In places where the raw edges of the seam are subject to wear or may fray, neaten them, using one of the techniques described on page 144.

There are also several flat seams which can be used to give a neatly finished edge in cases where the seam will get a lot of wear. The seams can be made so that the raw ends are encased and stitched down, to avoid the need for finishing the seams separately and to do away with awkward lumps and bumps. The choice depends on the strength of seam wanted, whether or not it has to lie flat and whether or not stitching on the right side will detract from the over-all look of the article.

BASIC FLAT SEAM

First, pin the two pieces of fabric with raw edges matching, placing the pins at right angles to the raw edges, spacing them at regular intervals down the line of the seam (Fig. 1).

Next, tack (baste) down the seamline (a marked or imaginary line 1.5cm ($\frac{1}{2}$in) from the raw edge of the fabric), removing the pins as you go (Fig. 2).

Finally, stitch by machine beside but not over the line of tacking (basting), starting 1cm ($\frac{1}{2}$in) from the end of the seam and making a few reverse stitches to the end of the seam (Fig. 3) to give a firm finish. At the other end of the seam, stitch backwards for 1cm ($\frac{1}{2}$in) again. Remove tacking (basting).

Press the seam from the wrong side of the fabric to blend the stitches into the fabric (Fig. 4).

Then open the seam flat and press the seam allowances down (Fig. 5), unless there are other special instructions and you want the bulk of the seam to lie in one direction.

STITCHING HINTS

Generally, stitch *down* the length of a seam (from the top of a curtain towards the hem, from the head of a bedspread towards the foot). One exception is stitching a gently curved or sloping seam. In this case, stitch as in Fig. 1 opposite to avoid pulling the fabric out of shape (Fig. 2).

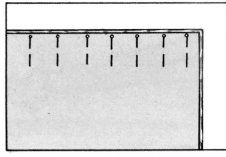

1. Pin fabric together as shown.

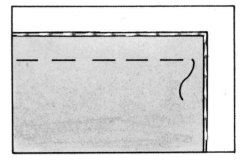

2. Tack (baste) down seam line.

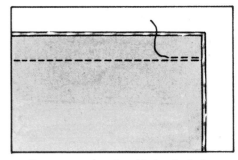

3. Secure seam ends with backstitch.

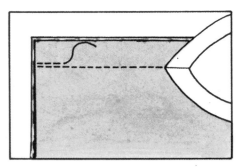

4. Press finished seam.

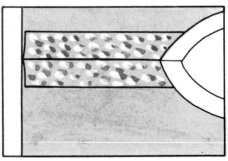

5. Press seam open flat.

Special fabrics

Pile. Make sure that the nap (the direction in which the pile lies) runs the same way on each side of the seam as far as possible. Stitch *with* the nap rather than against it.

You may find that, using heavier pile fabrics, the pile gets caught in the seam. Ease the pile out with a pin or the point of a needle for a neat finish (Fig. 3).

With heavier pile fabrics, trim the pile within the seam allowance before stitching the seam to eliminate unnecessary bulk (Fig. 4).

Fine fabrics. When stitching very fine fabrics (such as nylon net used for sheer curtains) the layers of fabric tend to slip. In this case, cut a strip or strips of tissue paper to run along the length of the seam and stitch the seam with a layer of tissue paper between the two pieces of fabric. After completing the stitching, the paper can be torn away (Fig. 5).

Vinyls and leather. These materials also need special care. Ensure that you do not pin or tack the fabric where the holes will show on the right side of the fabric. If you cannot pin or tack within the seam allowance, use paper clips or adhesive tape to hold the fabric while stitching it.

Trimming

To eliminate unnecessary bulk from seams, it is often a good idea to trim the seam allowances. This involves cutting the 1.5cm ($\frac{1}{2}$in) seam allowance to half its original width (Fig. 6).

Grading involves cutting one seam allowance even closer to the stitching. It is only necessary when both seam allowances are pressed to one side rather than being opened flat. The allowance which will lie uppermost is left wider to give a smoother effect on the right side. Grading is useful where there are more than two seam allowances in the seam, for example on a seam with piping running along it (Fig. 7).

Corners

When joining two flat pieces of fabric to make a right-angled corner (for example on a cushion cover), machine straight to the corner. Ensure that the needle is in the fabric at the point of the corner seam, then lift the presser foot, turn the fabric through 90° and continue stitching down the next side of the angle (Fig. 8a and b).

Trim the corner by cutting across it (Fig. 9).

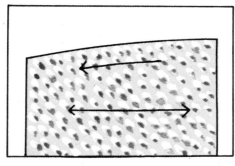

1. Stitch towards the tapered end.

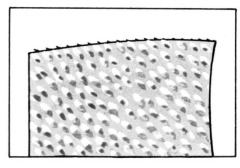

2. This prevents distortion.

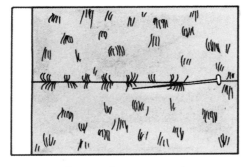

3. Ease pile out of seam.

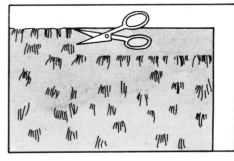

4. Trim heavy pile on seam allowance.

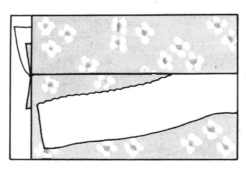

5. Use tissue paper between fine fabric.

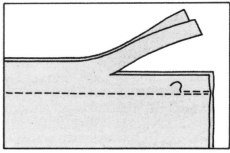

6. Trim unnecessary bulk from seam.

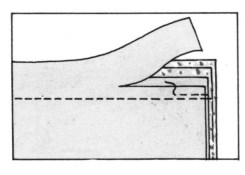

7. Grade or layer seam allowances.

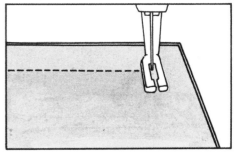

8a. Turn corner with needle in fabric.

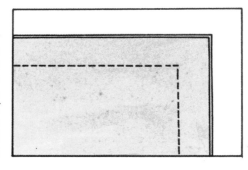

8b. Continue stitching down next side.

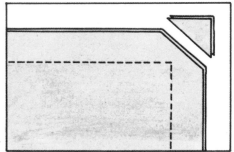

9. Clip corner for a tidy finish.

Sharp corner. For a corner which is sharper than 90°, make one, two or three stitches across the point of the corner, depending on the thickness of the fabric (Fig. 10).

Trim the corner as shown in Fig. 11.

Joining straight strip to corner.
Joining a straight strip of fabric to a flat right-angled piece of fabric to form a box shape (for example when making welted cushions) is a little more tricky. Pin and tack (baste) the strip to the flat piece as far as the corner. At the corner, clip into the seam allowance of the strip (Fig. 12). For a neat corner, this clip must match the point of the corner exactly. Continue to pin and tack (baste) round the other side of the angle.

Stitch the pieces together in one movement, turning the corner as for a right-angled corner.

Curves

In order to make curved seams lie flat, clip or notch the curved edge, depending on whether it is an outward or an inward curve (Fig. 13).

The sharper the curve, the closer together the clips or notches should be.

Finishing flat seams

Zigzag stitch. One of the simplest and quickest ways of finishing any seam is to stitch a row of zigzag stitches along the raw edges of the fabric (Fig. 14).

Oversewing. To achieve a similar effect by hand, see oversewing (overcasting) page 155.

Pinking. If the fabric is not very liable to fray, pinking or stitching and pinking, are possible finishes (Fig. 15). For stitching and pinking or hand oversewing, run a line of machine-stitching down the seam allowance about 7mm ($\frac{3}{8}$in) from the seam and trim the allowance before finishing.

Binding with straight seam binding is an alternative for bulky fabrics. (Fig. 16).

A self-bound seam is particularly useful where there is extra bulk, for example where a gathered frill is added to a flat section, and both seam allowances are pressed in the same direction.

Trim the seam allowance of the gathered section (Fig. 17). Turn under 5mm ($\frac{1}{4}$in) along the untrimmed seam allowance; press. Fold the turning over the trimmed seam allowance and slipstitch along the line of machine stitching (Fig. 18).

Turning and stitching gives a tidy finish on fairly fine fabrics (Fig. 19).

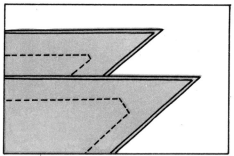

10. *Stitching round sharp corners.*

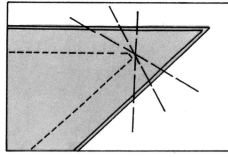

11. *Trim corner at chosen angles.*

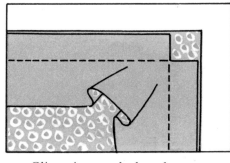

12. *Clip strip to make boxed corner.*

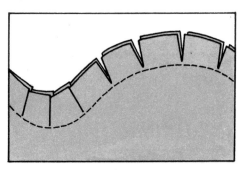

13. *Clip outward and notch inward curves.*

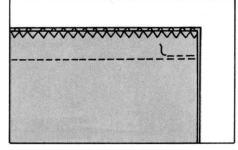

14. *Zigzag stitching is easiest finish.*

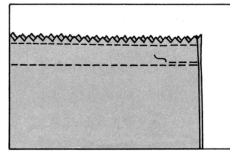

15. *Pink firmly woven fabrics.*

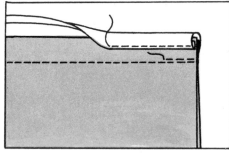

16. *Bind bulky fabric with seam binding.*

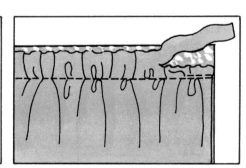

17. *For self-bound seam, trim one layer.*

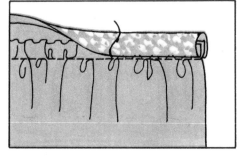

18. *Turn untrimmed edge over trimmed one.*

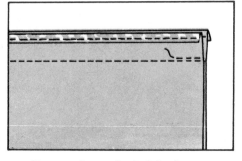

19. *Turn under and stitch both turnings.*

FRENCH SEAM

This seam gives a totally enclosed finish with no lines of stitching showing on the right side of the fabric. It is very hard-wearing and is often used for pillow-cases, shoe bags, laundry bags and so on. It is more suitable for seams in bags than for joining widths of fabric because it is not flat on the inside.

With wrong sides together and raw edges matching, stitch a seam 5mm (¼in) from the fabric edge (Fig. 1). Press. Trim edges slightly. Remove lines of tacking (basting) (Fig. 2).

Turn the seam back on itself and stitch another seam 10mm (⅜in) from the first seam (Fig. 3). This time, the fabric is stitched with right sides together, along the seamline. Press and turn seam to right side (Fig. 4).

MOCK FRENCH SEAM

This is similar to the French seam when finished, but is constructed in a slightly different way. It is easier to sew when there are a lot of corners or joins between seams.

Make a seam 1.5cm (½in) from the raw edges of the fabric, right sides together (Fig. 5). Turn in 5mm (¼in) down each seam allowance, folding the turnings towards each other. Stitch through both folds of the seam allowance, enclosing the raw edges (Fig. 6).

FLAT FELL SEAM

This seam gives a flatter finish than a French seam, but one or two lines of stitching show on the right side of the fabric. It is used when joining raw edges for bedspreads and so on, when a strong seam with well-enclosed allowances is wanted. It is a particularly hard-wearing seam.

To give two parallel rows of stitching on the right side, with wrong sides together and raw edges matching, make a seam 1.5cm (½in) from edges (Fig. 1). Press both seam allowances to one side. Following Fig. 2, trim the lower seam allowance to 3mm (⅛in) and turn under 5mm (¼in) down the upper seam allowance and press (Fig. 3).

Stitch the upper seam allowance to the main fabric so that the trimmed edge lies in the fold of the upper seam allowance. Stitch close to the edge of the fold (Fig. 4).

To show only one stitch line on the right side, this seam can also be made 'inside out', by stitching the first seam with right sides together.

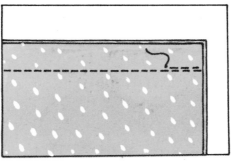

1. French seam : join fabric, wrong sides together. Stitch 5mm (¼in) from edge.

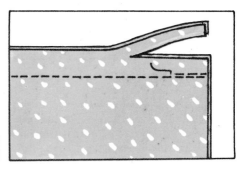

2. Trim seam allowances slightly, if necessary, to reduce bulk.

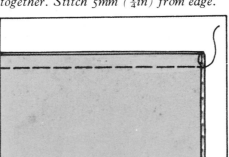

3. Turn fabric so that right sides face, tack (baste) 1cm (⅜in) from seamline.

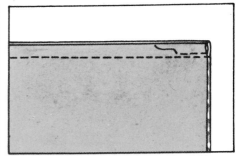

4. Stitch by machine, enclosing raw edges as indicated.

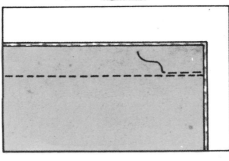

5. Mock French seam : flat seam first.

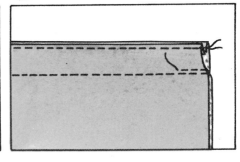

6. Turn in seam allowances and stitch.

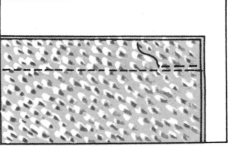

1. Flat fell seam : stitch seam first.

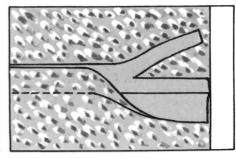

2. Trim one seam allowance.

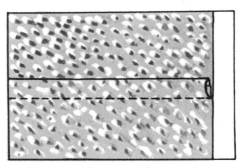

3. Turn one edge over trimmed edge.

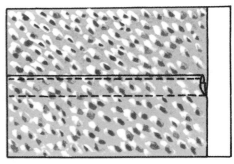

4. Stitch along fold for a flat seam.

145

LAPPED SEAM

This is similar to the flat fell seam but has the advantage that the first line of stitching is sewn from the right side so that it is possible to match patterns on printed and woven fabrics. It is particularly suitable when one of the edges to be joined is a selvedge.

Turn under 5mm ($\frac{1}{4}$in) down one raw edge (not the selvedge if there is one). Press.

With right sides upwards, lap this folded edge over the seam allowance of the other piece of fabric so that at least 1.5cm ($\frac{1}{2}$in) is covered. Pin and tack (baste) – making sure pattern matches on each side of join – and stitch the seam from the right side, through three layers of fabric (Fig. 1). Press.

Stitch the lower raw edge (or selvedge) to the upper layer of fabric, thus enclosing the folded-under raw edge (Fig. 2).

WELT SEAM

This is similar to the lapped seam, but it does not have the advantage of being sewn from the right side, so matching patterns is not so easy. Only one line of stitching shows on the right side of the fabric.

Again, it is suitable for use when one of the seam allowances is a selvedge.

Make a seam by stitching 1.5cm ($\frac{1}{2}$in) from the edges of the seam allowance, right sides together. Press both seam allowances to one side and trim the lower seam allowance to 5mm ($\frac{1}{4}$in) as in Fig. 1.

Stitch the upper seam allowance to the main fabric, thus enclosing the trimmed raw edge and producing a stitch line on fabric right side. (Fig. 2).

TOPSTITCHED SEAM

This gives a decorative and fairly firm finish to a flat seam, but it is not so hardwearing as some of the seams described here.

Stitch a flat seam as usual. Press both seam allowances to one side (Fig. 1) and on the right side stitch through all three layers of fabric (Fig. 2).

DOUBLE TOPSTITCHED SEAM

Another variation on the basic flat seam, the double topstitched seam, gives a trim finish which is flatter than the topstitched seam.

Begin by making a flat seam. Then press open (Fig. 1) and, on the right side, topstitch each seam allowance to the main fabric (Fig. 2). In both cases, the lines of topstitching should be about 5mm ($\frac{1}{4}$in) from the seamline.

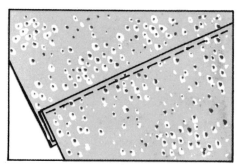
1. Lapped seam: turn under 5mm ($\frac{1}{4}$in) and lap fold over edge.

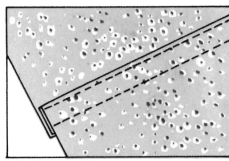
2. Make a second line of stitching, thus enclosing the raw edge.

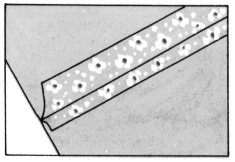
1. Welt seam: make a flat seam with right sides together. Trim one turning.

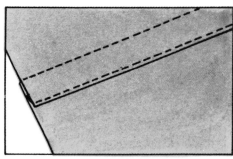
2. Press both turnings to one side. Stitch selvedge edge to enclose other.

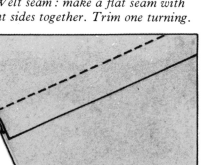
1. Topstitched seam: press to one side.

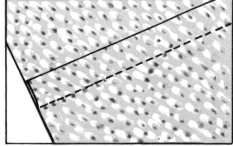
2. Stitch through both allowances.

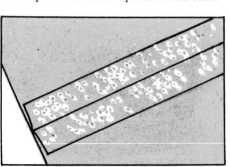
1. Double topstitch: press turnings open.

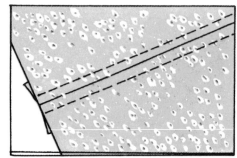
2. Topstitch each turning separately.

Hems and Edgings

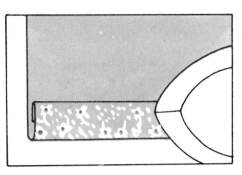

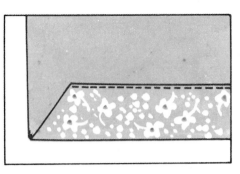

1. Turn under and press hem allowances.

2. Stitch by hand or machine.

PLAIN HEM

A hem is made by folding an edge of fabric over twice to prevent fraying and to give firmness. Most hems are made with turnings of uneven widths – perhaps by folding 1cm (⅜in) first and then 2cm (¾in). However, in cases where the edge of the first turning might form a ridge, and where the hem allowance is very deep, it is better to make the turnings of equal width.

Fold over half, or less than half, the hem allowance to the wrong side and press. Fold over the remaining hem allowance and press again (Fig. 1). Mitre the corners (This is described in detail on page 151.) Baste the hem in position and stitch by machine (Fig. 2) or slipstitch by hand as described on page 154.

HEMSTITCHED HEM

Use to give subtle decorative finish along edges where the hemline follows the fabric weave. Choose fabric which has firm threads which may be pulled out easily.

Allow enough fabric to give equal first and second turnings in the hem. Before turning the hem, measure inwards one and a half times the total hem allowance. Mark spot with tacking threads.

Lift and cut the next fabric thread which lies parallel to the edge at this point (Fig. 1).

Using the point of a pin, and working back to the corners of the hem, carefully pull out the cut thread. If making hems all round, as on a tablecloth, pull out thread along each edge until they meet at the corners. Cut off drawn threads, leaving 1.5cm (½in). Repeat with three or four more threads, working inwards (Fig. 2).

Continue as for a plain hem, placing the first fold level with the first drawn thread of the border (Fig. 3). Tuck the cut ends under the hem and secure with tiny back stitches, then work hemstitching (Fig. 4) all round to secure the hem and decorate the border.

1. Draw out cut thread.

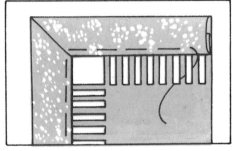

2. Leave 1.5cm (½in) at corners.

3. Turn in a double hem.

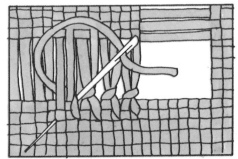

4. To secure threads, stitch hem over folded edge of fabric, grouping remaining threads in border with hemstitch.

FRILLS

Decide the finished width and add either a seam and hem allowance or, for narrow frills which are most easily made double, add a seam allowance and double the total.

Cut strips on the straight grain to the calculated width by 1½–2 times the length of the edge to which the frill is to be attached.

If making a continuous frill (for a cushion or pillowcase), join the short ends of the strip together. If you want a hem along the outer edge, stitch it now. Otherwise fold the frill in half lengthwise and with right sides out; treat the double fabric as if single from now on.

Divide the free edge of the frill and that of the main fabric in half and then into quarters. Work two rows of gathering stitches (using a long machine stitch or a hand running stitch) on the frill, placing one row inside the seamline and one row outside it (Fig. 1). On long edges it is advisable to work these rows in sections to avoid breaking threads.

With right sides together, pin the frill to the main fabric so that sections correspond. Pull the gathering threads together so that the frill fits the edge and arrange gathers evenly (Fig. 2).

Stitch along the seamline. Pull out the gathering threads completely. Neaten the edges.

BIAS BINDING

Bias binding has many uses in home sewing. It may be bought commercially cut and folded ready for use, or you can cut it from the fabric you are using, or a contrasting fabric. The advantage of *bias* binding is that it has more give and is therefore more flexible than binding cut on the straight grain.

Its main uses are to add finishing touches – either when used to bind the raw edges of fabric (particularly quilted fabric which is difficult to turn and hem in the usual way), or when used to cover piping to add a neat trim to a seam.

Cutting bias binding. Find the bias (as opposed to straight) grain of the fabric by folding a raw edge cut straight across the grain of the fabric parallel with selvedge of fabric (Fig. 1). The fold line is on the bias. To make the bias binding, cut strips parallel to this fold line (Fig. 2).

For narrow bindings decide on the finished width and multiply by four.

For wider bindings, double finished width and add 1.5cm (½in) for seam

turnings of 5mm (¼in) on each edge. As a general rule strips 2.5cm (1in) wide are sufficient for most purposes. Strips 4cm (1½in) wide are suitable for making piping, but it is worth testing a small sample with the cord being used before cutting out a lot of strips.

Joining strips. It is usually necessary to join strips of binding to make a sufficient length. This is done by making flat seams on the straight grain of the fabric. This means that the short ends of the strips will be on the straight grain.

Mark seamlines 5mm (¼in) from the raw edges on the two pieces to be joined. These two seamlines should overlap exactly, leaving triangular corners.

Pin and stitch the seam (Fig. 3). Open the seam out flat, press and trim the corners (Fig. 4).

Folding binding. If the binding is to be used for neatening edges, for example on table linen or bedspreads, it is easier to use if it is pre-folded. Mark a line 5mm (¼in) from each raw edge of the strip on the wrong side of the fabric. Fold down these lines and press firmly (Fig. 5). When you come to use the binding, these fold lines will be the stitching lines.

Cutting continuous strips. If you need a long strip of binding and do not want to join strips, there is a method of joining them *before* cutting them.

Find the bias of a rectangle of material as described earlier. Mark the line and cut down it (BE in Fig. 6).

Join one edge of the triangle you have cut off (AB) to the opposite edge of the rectangle (DC) (Fig. 7) and mark the bias strips across the re-shaped piece of fabric (see Fig. 7).

Next, join the two sides of the fabric together, matching the top point of the left-hand side to the first mark down the right-hand side and the lower point of the right-hand side to the lowest mark on the left-hand side. This gives a tube with the cutting line marked continuously (Fig. 8).

Binding edges

To bind the edge of a piece of fabric, open one folded edge of the bias binding and match the raw edge to the raw edge of the fabric, right sides together. Pin and stitch down the fold line of the binding (Fig. 9).

Refold the binding and turn it over to the wrong side of the fabric being bound.

Pin and slipstitch (or machine stitch) the second folded edge to the main

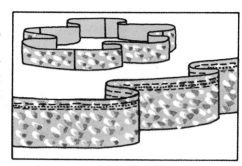

1. Work two lines of gathering stitch.

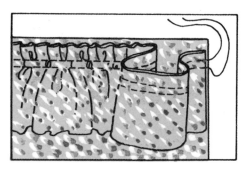

2. Draw up and distribute gathers.

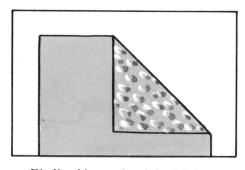

1. Finding bias grain of the fabric.

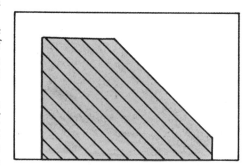

2. Mark parallel cutting lines.

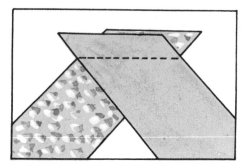

3. Join fabric lengths, stitching 5mm (¼in) from the raw edges. Note the angles this seam produces.

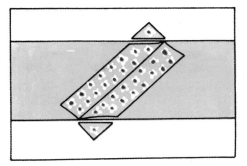

4. Press seam open. Clip corners.

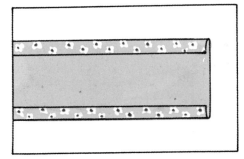

5. Press under turnings.

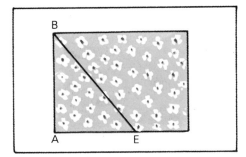

6. Mark bias on a rectangle.

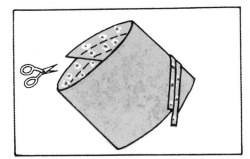

7. Join edges. Mark cutting lines.

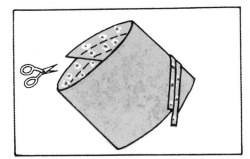

8. Join opposite edges, staggering cutting lines. Cut along these to make continuous strips.

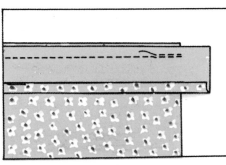

9. Stitch binding to right side of fabric.

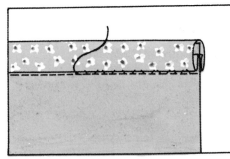

10. Turn to wrong side and slipstitch.

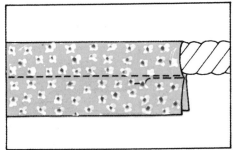

1. Fold fabric over piping and stitch.

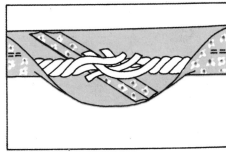

2. Joining lengths of piping.

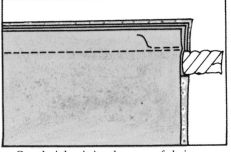

3. Sandwich piping between fabric, right sides facing, raw edges matching. Stitch together as shown.

fabric down the first line of stitching (Fig. 10).

PIPING

Piping, made by covering cord with fabric, is often applied to prominent seams in soft furnishing as decoration and to add strength, as it prevents the seamline from becoming worn by continual chafing.

The fabric strip is cut with extra width so that flaps may be sewn into the seam as it is formed. The fabric should always be cut on the bias, so that it moulds easily around the cord. It may be made from the same fabric as the item being made or a contrasting fabric can be used.

Cord for use in piping can be bought in different sizes and materials. A fine synthetic fabric needs fine synthetic cord and thick cotton fabric (e.g. velvet) needs thick cotton cord. Check that it is pre-shrunk. If not, put it in a saucepan of boiling water and simmer for three minutes, then drain and dry thoroughly before use.

Making piping. Lay the cord down the centre of the wrong side of the bias strip (see details opposite for making bias strips). Fold the strip in half. Pin and tack (baste) the strip with wrong sides together and raw edges matching. Stitch down the strip as close to the cord as possible (Fig. 1). If machine stitching, use the special piping foot attachment.

Trim seam allowance to 1.5cm (½in).

Joining piping. Piping should be joined to form a continuous piece before being used. The bias strips are joined as described previously. In order to make a smooth join in the piping itself, unravel a couple of centimetres (about an inch) at each end. Trim each of the three strands making up the cord to different lengths and then twist them round each other as shown (Fig. 2).

Using piping cord

The piping is sewn into the seam as you stitch the main seamline. If the seam is straightforward, this can be done with just one line of stitching, through the two pieces of fabric being joined with the piping sandwiched in the middle (Fig. 3). In some cases (for example, welted cushions) it is easier to stitch the piping to one piece of fabric first, then make main seam.

The raw edges of the piping should always match the raw edges of the sections being stitched. Grade the seam allowances after stitching (see page 143).

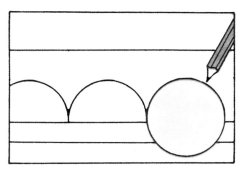

1. Make a template from paper by drawing round a saucer.

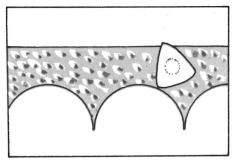

2. Mark scallops on fabric by drawing round pattern with dressmaker's chalk.

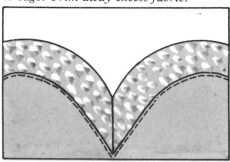

3. Zigzag stitch round scallops, close to edge. Trim away excess fabric.

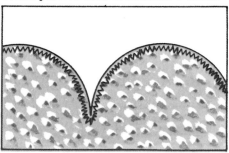

4. To attach bias binding, mitre fullness between scallops.

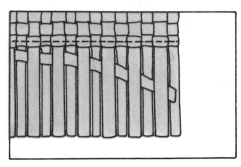

1. For a self-fabric fringe, machine down seamline. Draw out threads individually.

150

SCALLOPS

Scalloped edges can be finished by decorative stitching, by binding or with a facing.

For all methods, make a paper pattern to fit the edge to be scalloped and draw the design required, using a template such as a saucer (Fig. 1). Place the pattern on the fabric and draw round the edge (Fig. 2). Add 5mm ($\frac{1}{4}$in) seam allowance if finishing with a facing.

Decorative stitching. Work zig-zagging or blanket stitching along the drawn pattern line and trim away the excess fabric (Fig. 3).

Binding. Cut along the seamline and attach bias binding, mitring the full-ness between scallops.

Facing. Cut a strip of fabric to the same shape as the edge and attach as described opposite for facing.

GATHERING

This is described in detail under 'frills' on page 148.

The fabric to be gathered should be $1\frac{1}{2}$–2 times longer than the edge to which it is being attached.

Place gathering stitches in two rows, 5mm ($\frac{1}{4}$in) apart, on either side of the seamline. To work the stitches, use either a hand running stitch or a long machine stitch with tight bobbin tension.

FRINGES

Self fringes are made by fraying threads along the edge of the fabric. Decide the depth of fringe and add this amount when measuring the fabric.

Machine stitch along the seamline (where the fringe will begin) and then, working from the lower edge upwards, pull out one fabric thread at a time up to the line (Fig. 1).

Bought fringing. Buy fringing to the length of the edge to which it is being attached plus 10mm ($\frac{1}{2}$in).

If applying it in a straight, flat length, fold under each raw end for 5mm ($\frac{1}{4}$in) and slipstitch neatly.

If applying it in a continuous piece, stitch the ends together taking 5mm ($\frac{1}{4}$in) turnings. Press the turnings open and oversew neatly to the wrong side of the main piece.

Trim the seam allowance of the fabric edge to slightly less than the depth of the fringe heading and, with wrong sides together, stitch the lower edge of the fringe heading to the seamline of the fabric.

Turn the heading up on the right side of the fabric and stitch the upper edge to the fabric.

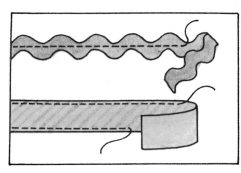

1. Machine stitch braid in place.

APPLYING BRAIDS

Narrow braids. Mark the position required on the right side of the fabric with tailor's chalk, place the braid centrally over it and machine stitch along its length (Fig. 1a).

Wide braids. Mark and position as narrow braids but machine stitch or slipstitch along both edges (Fig. 1b).

APPLYING CORD

Allow a length of cord to fit the edge to which it is being attached plus 2.5cm (1in).

If applying to a single straight edge, place the cord end on the wrong side and secure with two or three over-sewing stitches.

If applying to the perimeter of a cushion cover, for example, leave a small gap in the stitching near one corner during making up and insert the end into it. Sew the cord on in matching thread by passing the needle through the cord and taking tiny stitches along the seamline (Fig. 1). Attach the end in the same way as the beginning.

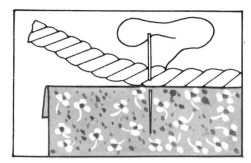

1. Stitch through cord and attach it with tiny stitches to fold of seamline.

Special techniques

FACING AND REVERSE FACING

A facing is a piece of fabric cut to match the edge of another piece of fabric (such as the scalloped head of a curtain), and stitched in place to neaten the raw edge.

To face a straight edge, cut strips of fabric on the straight grain to the finished length and width plus seam allowances.

To face a shaped edge, place the edge on paper, or directly on the fabric to be used, and draw round the curve to be faced with a pencil or with tailor's chalk, allowing extra for a seam allowance on the inner edge (Fig. 1).

Mark the required depth (width) of the facing, using dressmaker's carbon to trace it on the paper or facing fabric (see Fig. 1) and a ruler or compass to measure the curve evenly. Then cut along outer marks to form facing shape. Place the facing on the main fabric with right sides together for a concealed finish, or with wrong sides together, if you wish the facing to form a border. Mitre any corners and stitch along the seam line.

Trim the seam allowances to 5mm (¼in) and clip or notch curves. Turn the facing to the opposite side of the fabric and press carefully so that the seamline lies along the edge (Fig. 2).

Turn under the free edge of the facing and machine or slipstitch to the main fabric.

MITRING

Mitring is the technique of neatening fabric ends at corners. The exact method depends on the type of corner and whether it is the fabric itself being neatened or a lace or broderie anglaise trim or braid appliqué.

Mitring a hem on an outward corner

Fold under 5mm (¼in) down each edge to be hemmed.

Fold in the corner so that the diagonal fold meets the fold lines of the hem as shown (Fig. 1) and cut off the corner, leaving a 5mm (¼in) seam allowance. Turn in the hems down the fold lines and stitch down. Slipstitch the diagonal seam (Fig. 2).

Mitring a hem on an inward corner

For extra strength, staystitch (stitch with machine stitches) along the fold line of the hem around the corner to be mitred. Clip into the turning at the corner, clipping to the line of staystitching (Fig. 3).

Turn in the hems and stitch as usual.

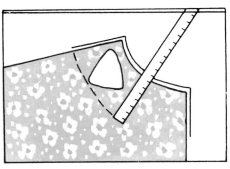

1. Choose depth of facing and mark with tailor's chalk and carbon.

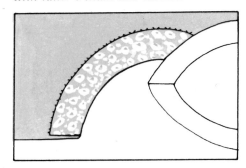

2. Turn facing to inside and press.

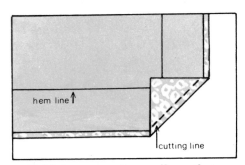

1. Fold the corner diagonally so that diagonal fold meets fold of hem.

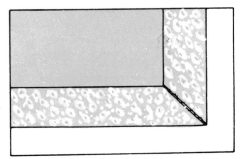

2. Fold in hems and slipstitch together.

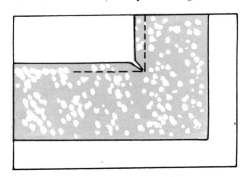

3. For an inward corner, such as a cut out panel, staystitch foldline of hem around corner to be mitred.

151

Mitring broderie anglaise trim

Cut the broderie anglaise to match each side of the angle, allowing an overlap equal to the depth of the trim plus a seam allowance of 5mm ($\frac{1}{4}$in). Stitch the broderie anglaise in place to within a short distance of the corner (Fig. 4). Trim diagonally across the two pieces of broderie anglaise as indicated, leaving a small seam allowance.

Make a seam diagonally across the broderie anglaise, 5mm ($\frac{1}{4}$in) from the raw edges. Stitch the broderie anglaise to the main fabric where it was left unstitched before (Fig. 5).

Press the trim outwards. Neaten the raw edges of the trim on the wrong side at the corners by oversewing (overcasting) (Fig. 6).

Mitring braid trim

Decorative braid is often applied to curtains, cushions, bedspreads and so on, and where it is applied parallel to the edge of the article it may be necessary to mitre it at the corners.

Fold the braid back on itself, right sides together (Fig. 7). To obtain a seam line, fold the folded edge up to the braid selvedge as indicated in Fig. 7 and crease it to form a stitching line.

Stitch diagonally across folded braid along the crease and then trim off edges 5mm ($\frac{1}{4}$in) from the stitching (Fig. 8). Press seam open, clip corners which protrude beyond the braid and open braid out before applying it to the article being decorated.

Apply, as described previously, by stitching along both long edges (Fig. 9).

CALCULATING PATTERNED FABRICS

If using patterned fabric which is narrower than your requirements, it must be joined so that the pattern matches at the seam.

To calculate the amount of fabric necessary to do this, first check the size of the pattern repeat. Then decide how many widths of fabric are needed by dividing the total width (including seam allowances) by the fabric width. Round up the answer to make a whole number.

Example: 200cm ÷ 122cm = 2 (rounded up)

Divide the total length by the pattern repeat and round up to make a whole number. Allow this number of pattern repeats to the length.

Example: 80 ÷ 12 = 7 (rounded up)

Multiply the number of pattern repeats by the number of fabric widths required.

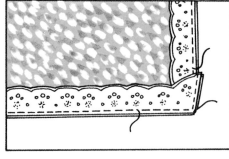

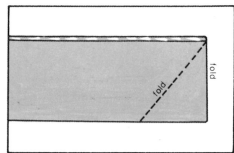

4. *Stitch broderie anglaise almost to corner. Trim lace diagonally.*

5. *Make a seam joining trimmed ends of broderie anglaise.*

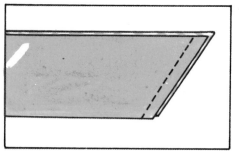

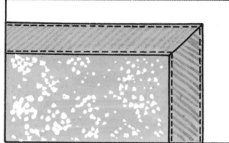

6. *Press flat, oversew raw edges.*

7. *Fold braid, right sides together.*

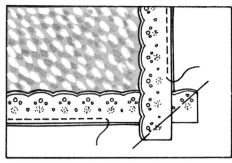

8. *Stitch at angles as shown, then cut off corner of fabric.*

9. *Open braid and press seam flat, trim, then sew to main fabric.*

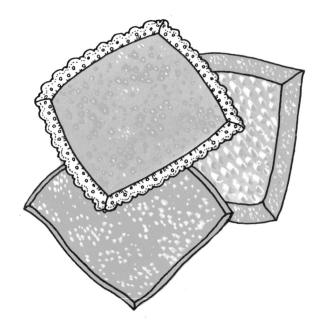

ZIP FASTENERS

Zip fasteners are often used to make unobtrusive closures for chair covers, cushions and so on.

Centred zip

This method of application involves making equal hems on either side of the zip. It is much easier to put in the zip if the sections of fabric being joined are not made up; putting in a zip should be one of the first steps in making up an article.

Stitch a flat seam, leaving a gap for the position of the zip, and press the seam allowances open along both the stitched and the unstitched sections.

From the right side, roughly slipstitch the opening together along the folded edges. Centre the zip under the opening (Fig. 1). Pin and tack (baste) in place, positioning the lines of stitching 3mm (⅛in) from the teeth of the zip.

Using a zip foot on the sewing machine, topstitch the zip in place from the right side of the fabric, and stitch across the tape ends of the zip to join the lines of topstitching, stitching as close as possible to the ends of the zip itself (Fig. 2).

If you are putting in the zip by hand, stitch with prickstitch (see page 155).

Lapped zip

This insertion is used where the seam allowances of the seam in which the zip is set are pressed in one direction. It is usually used where one end of the zip is open.

The seam allowances down the section of the seam where the zip is inserted should be the same width as the zip itself, including the tape.

Match one edge of the zip tape to the raw edge of the underlapping fabric. Pin and tack (baste) in position down the side of the zip away from that raw edge. Stitch down, positioning the stitching 3mm (⅛in) from the teeth of the zip (Fig. 3).

Fold under the seam allowance down the other raw edge to be joined. Match the fold to the edge of the tape down the side of the zip which has already been stitched. Pin, tack (baste) and topstitch the folded edge to the unstitched side of the zip, being careful not to stitch through the underlap of the other seam allowance; this is easier if the zip is open. Finally, close the zip and topstitch across the tape ends at the foot of the zip to meet the seamline (Fig. 4).

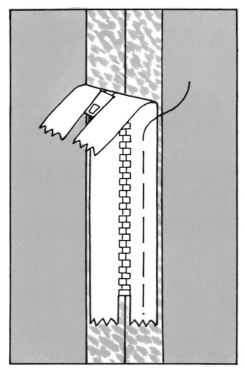

1. Position zip centrally over gap left in seam. Tack (baste) in place.

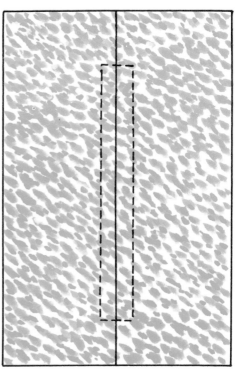

2. Topstitch using zip foot attachment or prickstitch, and secure end tapes.

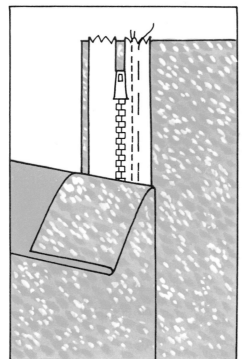

3. Match one edge of zip to raw edge of underlapping fabric. Stitch down the opposite edge.

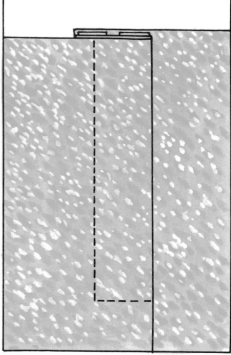

4. Stitch other side to overlapping fabric. Topstitch across the bottom of the zip through both layers of fabric.

Hand sewing

TACKING (BASTING)

These terms refer to temporary stitching used to hold fabric in position while the permanent stitching is done. Work from right to left if you are right handed.

Secure thread end with a knot. Make stitches 5mm–1cm ($\frac{1}{4}$–$\frac{1}{2}$in) long where the permanent stitching is to be placed (Fig. 1).

Always remove tacking stitches when permanent stitching is complete.

SLIPSTITCH

This is used to hold a folded edge to a flat edge or to hold two folded edges together. It may be worked from the right side of the fabric, and is worked from right to left, if right-handed.

Secure the end of the thread by making a couple of stitches on top of each other. (This is the way to secure the thread for all the following hand stitches.)

Take a small stitch inside the folded edge, sliding the needle along inside the fold for about 5mm ($\frac{1}{4}$in). Bring the needle out of the fold and insert it into the other piece of fabric exactly opposite the point where it came out. Catch a couple of threads from the opposite piece of fabric (Fig. 2).

Bring the needle out of the fabric and draw up the thread. Repeat the process, inserting the needle into the fold opposite the point where you brought it out before.

HEMMING

This is used to hold a folded edge to flat fabric. It is worked from the wrong side of the fabric (over a fold to the wrong side) and is normally worked from right to left.

With the folded edge towards you, hold the needle above the hem, pointing diagonally from right to left. Pick up a couple of threads from the flat piece of fabric. Bring the needle under the folded edge and up through the two layers of fabric. Repeat the process a little way to the left (Fig. 3).

CATCHSTITCH

This is used like hemming but is a more suitable finish for bulky fabrics or curved hems. It is worked from the wrong side, from left to right.

With the needle pointing right to left, take a stitch through the flat layer of fabric, picking up just a couple of threads. Move the needle to the right and take a stitch, again right to left, through the folded edge of the fabric (Fig. 4).

Repeat to give a herringbone effect.

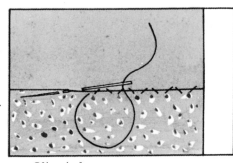

1. Tacking (basting)

2. Slipstitch

3. Hemming

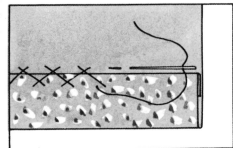

4. Catchstitch

BACKSTITCH

This stitch gives a very secure join and is the hand sewing substitute for ordinary machine stitch. It is worked from right to left if you are right handed.

Take a stitch under the fabric, from right to left, then bring the needle back and take another stitch, the same length, starting from half way along the first stitch. Repeat, inserting the point of the needle at the end of the previous stitch each time (Fig. 5).

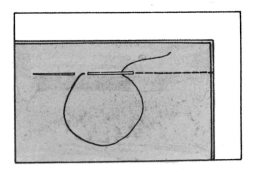

5. Backstitch

PRICKSTITCH

This is similar to backstitch but is worked from the right side as the finished line of stitches is unobtrusive. It is often used for inserting zips.

For each stitch, insert the needle just to the right of the point where the needle came out of the fabric, so that only a few threads are caught down and the stitch is very small (Fig. 6).

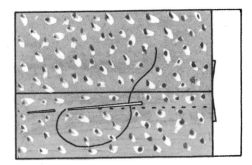

6. Prickstitch

OVERSEWING (OVERCASTING)

The main use for this stitch is to neaten raw edges.

It simply involves taking the thread over the edge of the fabric, bringing the needle through from the back each time (Fig. 7).

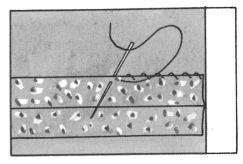

7. Oversewing (overcasting)

BLANKET STITCH

This gives a more secure and more decorative finish to a raw edge. It is usually worked over a folded edge.

Secure the thread at the top of the folded edge. Insert the needle about 5mm ($\frac{1}{4}$in) from the left edge, below the edge of the fold. Point the needle straight up and loop the thread over behind the point. Draw the thread up so that it lies neatly along the top of the fold (Fig. 8).

RUNNING STITCH

Use for hand gathering. Secure the thread at the beginning of the row and work the needle in and out of the fabric along the seamline, taking tiny stitches and leaving equal tiny spaces between them.

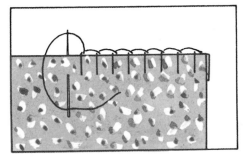

8. Blanket stitch

Index

Supply sources

UNITED KINGDOM

Designers Guild shops
277 and 271 Kings Road
London SW3

15 London Road
Alderley Edge
Cheshire

Designers Guild fabrics
are available from
the following retail outlets
and distributors:

AVON
Michael J. Bracey
35-37 Alma Vale Road
Clifton
Bristol B58 2HS

Coexistence
10 Argyle Street
Bath
Avon

BERKSHIRE
Dalrymple & Pettifer Ltd
94 High Street
Hungerford
Berkshire

BUCKINGHAM
Leitch Freeland
7 Whielden Street
Old Amersham
Buckingham

CAMBRIDGE
Joshua Taylor Ltd
Sidney Street
Cambridge

CHANNEL ISLANDS
Rory Ramsden
Tower Hill House
The Bordage
St. Peter Port
Guernsey
Channel Islands

DERBY
David David Designs
41 Church Street
Ashbourne
Derby

DEVON
Hatchetts Interiors
51 Old Butterwalk
High Street
Totnes
Devon

DORSET
G-Craft Limited
Walford Mill
Knobcrook Road
Wimborne
Dorset

Johnsons of Sherborne
South Street
Sherborne
Dorset

DURHAM
Arch Interiors
Coniscliffe House
Northumberland Street
Darlington
Co. Durham

EAST SUSSEX
Meeting House Interiors
6 Dukes Lane
Brighton
East Sussex

ESSEX
Gordon Powling
5 Spreadeagle
High Street
Ingatestone
Essex

GLOUCESTER
Roomours Design Limited
28/32 Winchcombe Street
Cheltenham
Gloucester GL52 2LY

GREATER LONDON
Another Maloneys
64 Tranquil Vale
Blackheath
London SE3 OBN

Tom Allan Interiors
38b High Street
Wimbledon Village
London SW19

Paper Moon
12 Kingswell
Heath Street
Hampstead
London NW3

Peacock
3 White Hart Lane
Barnes
London SW13

Harrods
Knightsbridge
London SW3

GREATER MANCHESTER
Wolff & Alexander
16 John Dalton Street
Manchester M2 6HT

HAMPSHIRE
Derek Walls
17 Latimer Street
Romsey
Hampshire SO5 8DF

HEREFORD & WORCESTER
Morgan & Oates
The House in the Yard
Church Lane
Ledbury
Hereford & Worcester

HERTFORD
Clement Joscelyne
Market Square
Bishops Stortford
Hertford

Designers Fountain
20 Heritage Close
St. Albans
Hertford

HUMBERSIDE
Marr of Beverley
4 North Bar Without
Beverley
Humberside

ISLE OF MAN
By Design Limited
3 The Quay
Ramsey
Isle of Man

KENT
Merlin Pennink
25-27 The Pantiles
Tunbridge Wells
Kent

LEICESTER
Harlequin Interior Design
23 Silver Street
Leicester

NORFOLK
The Decorating Shop
Roydon
Kings Lynn
Norfolk

NORTHAMPTON
Coles Furnishings
54 Gold Street
Northampton

NORTHERN IRELAND
D & L Interiors
29 Great Victoria Street
Belfast BT2 7AL
Northern Ireland

Inscape
80 High Street
Co. Down
Northern Ireland

NORTH YORKSHIRE
Woods of Harrogate
65-67 Station Parade
Harrogate
North Yorkshire

OXFORD
Mary S The Home Cook Shop
1 High Street
Goring on Thames
Oxford

SCOTLAND – FIFE
John McGregor
    of St. Andrews Ltd
73 Market Street
St. Andrews
Fife
Scotland

GRAMPIAN
Decor (Aberdeen) Ltd
157 Skene Street
Aberdeen ABI IQL
Grampian
Scotland

LOTHIAN
A. F. Drysdale
35 North West Circus Place
Edinburgh EH36 TW
Lothian
Scotland

STRATHCLYDE
Joni Ancill Interiors
West Sussex
Burnside Road
White Craigs
Glasgow
Strathclyde
Scotland

SOUTH YORKSHIRE
New Design
49 Church Street
Barnsley
South Yorkshire

Shape Design
16-18 Carver Street
Sheffield S14 FS
South Yorkshire

SUFFOLK
Sister Moon
Kirby House
20 The Thoroughfare
Woodbridge
Suffolk

SURREY
October House
High Street
Limpsfield
Surrey

Pipelines Indec
6/8 Post Boys Row
Between Streets
Cobham
Surrey

The Tarrystone
High Street
Chobham
Surrey

TYNE AND WEAR
Colin Clasper Ltd
11/12 Clayton Road
Jesmond
Newcastle on Tyne
Tyne and Wear

WALES – SOUTH GLAMORGAN
Monaghan Limited
4 Whitchurch Road
Cardiff
South Glamorgan
Wales

WEST MIDLANDS
Claude Hooper
63/65 Mill Lane
Solihull
West Midlands

Home Sweet Home
42 Queen Square
Wolverhampton
West Midlands

WEST SUSSEX
David and Carol Burkinshaw
    Interiors
66 High Street
Lindfield
West Sussex

Margaret Wilkinson Interiors
10 Eastgate Square
Chichester
West Sussex

AUSTRALIA

Piaff Interiors
29 Ranelagh Drive
Mt. Eliza
Victoria 3930
Australia

Poccomela
1025 High St.
Armadale
Melbourne
Australia

Decortex
Shop 1
181c Edgecliff Road
Woolahra
N.S.W.
Australia

John Glynn
Design House
116 Fifth Avenue
Windsor
Brisbane 4030
Queensland
Australia

BERMUDA

Hamma Galleries
39 Victoria Street
Hamilton
Bermuda

HONG KONG

Avant Garde Designs Ltd
202 Far East Exchange Building
Corner of 8 Wyndham Street
& On Lan Street Central
Hong Kong

CANADA

Telio & Cie
31 Dollard Place
Bonaventure CP 1261
Montreal
Canada

EIRE

Stock Design Ltd
33/34 South King Street
Dublin 2
Eire

CHANNEL ISLANDS

Insiders Ltd
7 Market Street
St. Helier
Jersey

Rory Ramsden Ltd
Tower Hill House
The Bordage
St. Peter Port
Guernsey

SOUTH AFRICA

Selwyn Neiman Pty.
Nedbank Hall 5th Floor
35 Siemert Road
Doornfontein
Johannesburg
South Africa

UNITED STATES OF AMERICA

Brunschwig & Fils
410 East 62nd Street
N.Y. 10021
New York
U.S.A.

Vice Versa
315 East 62nd Street
New York
U.S.A.

Acknowledgements

ILLUSTRATORS
Marion Appleton
Olivia Beasley
Barbara Firth
Wendy Jones
Coral Mula
Jill Shipley
ADDITIONAL PHOTOGRAPHY
Geoffrey Frosh
Jon Harris
SMALL THINGS
Lined baskets
by Muriel Mackenzie